Be Encouraged

Words of Encouragement that Will Change Your Outlook on Life

Be Encouraged

Words of Encouragement that Will Change Your Outlook on Life

If you would like more information about the encouragement ministry of Cerise Lewis or to schedule an Encouragement Seminar, please contact:

CERISE DIONE LEWIS
www.ceriselewis.com
booking@ceriselewis.com
Post Office Box 43217
Minneapolis, MN 55443

Published by Resurrecting Faith Publishing

Editor: Wanda Elliott and Cerise Lewis
Cover Illustration and Design: Teon Simmons & Luke Boynton

Unless otherwise indicated, all Scripture quotations are from the King James Version of the Bible.

Resurrecting Faith Publishing
PO Box 43217, Brooklyn Park, MN 55443
www.churchofminneapolis.org
admin@churchofminneapolis.org

Lewis, Cerise, 1972-
Be Encouraged
Words of Encouragement that Will Change Your Outlook on Life

ISBN 978-0-9729876-4-6
Printed in U.S.A on acid-free paper
Distributed by Resurrecting Faith Publishing

How to use this book:

This book is a tool designed to minister to the needs of women that are simply seeking encouragement and strength as well as women that may have a personal relationship with God. Scriptures are provided if you are interested in digging further into what the Bible says about each topic.

To benefit from this book, you should read one chapter each week, meditate on the chapter and understand what the chapter is saying to you. Take notes, write down points that speak to you and your situation, then, focus on the action steps for the week. Set your mind and your will to follow and do the action steps for the entire week. Make the necessary adjustments and changes you need to make so that you receive the empowerment from the steps that you are taking.

A companion journal is a complement to this book as you will have various exercises and thoughts to write down. Keeping them in one place allows for quick review. Take this book week by week and action step by action step. If you find something more challenging, do that chapter for two weeks rather than one. The purpose is that you receive power and strength from the changes that you make in your life and the encouragement that you get from the Word. Feel free to move around within the book to subjects that are fitting to your specific situations.

After completing this book, look over your life and your journal and see that you are not the same person you were when you started this book. You are very different. You are encouraged, strengthened and empowered to prosper in every area of your life!

Table of Contents

Week 1: Woman Where Are You 8
Week 2: Master Your Emotions 10
Week 3: You Can Do Anything 13
Week 4: You Are Forgiven 15
Week 5: You Must Have Expectation 17
Week 6: You Must Be Humble 19
Week 7: Don't Give Up 21
Week 8: Run Your Race 23
Week 9: God's Place in Your Life 25
Week 10: Completing Your Journey 27
Week 11: Your Challenges are Opportunities for Growth 29
Week 12: All Your Wounds Can be Healed 31
Week 13: Live Everyday Stress Free 33
Week 14: Your life is Redeemed from Destruction 35
Week 15: You Deserve Happiness in Your Life 37
Week 16: Simplify 39
Week 17: Slow Down Your Moving Too Fast 41
Week 18: Rest for Your Soul 49
Week 19: God's Grace is Sufficient for You 45
Week 20: God Loves You 47
Week 21: God's Standard 49
Week 22: An Ordered Life 51
Week 23: Your Wealthy Place 53
Week 24: Relationships 55
Week 25: Destined for Greatness 58
Week 26: Give up the Victim Mentality 60
Week 27: The Best is Yet to Come 62
Week 28: Purge Yourself 64
Week 29: Encouragement is... 66
Week 30: God Has Invested In You 68

Week 31: Passion on the Inside of You 70
Week 32: Stay Strong in the Lord 71
Week 33: Overcome Fear and Failure 72
Week 34: Exercise Your Faith 73
Week 35: Right Now Faith 74
Week 36: Love 76
Week 37: Money Isn't Everything 78
Week 38: Comfort Zones 80
Week 39: God is Faithful to You 82
Week 40: Trust in the Lord 83
Week 41: Your Relationship with God 84
Week 42: The Needful Thing 85
Week 43: Seek the Lord 86
Week 44: What is Woman? 88
Week 45: Do Not Settle For Second Best 89
Week 46: Set Boundaries 90
Week 47: You are a New Creature 92
Week 48: You Do Not Have to Be Depressed 94
Week 49: Thank the Lord 96
Week 50: Time & Enemies 98
Week 51: Accomplishments 100
Week 52: Set Goals and Achieve Them 101
Acknowledgements 103
About the Author 104

Be Encouraged

Words of Encouragement that Will Change Your Outlook on Life

I pray that you are encouraged by the Word of God for it is life to us!

Did you know that the Word of God is everything that we need to have a full and prosperous life? 2 Peter 1:3 says, "*According as His divine power hath given unto us all things that pertain unto life and godliness, through the knowledge of Him that hath called us to glory and virtue.*" The power of God is made available to us so that whatever we need, can be obtained.

The power given is for life and godliness, not selfish ambition or gain. This gift has been given because we have been called to excellence and glory. This gift is a tool to help us develop and become what God wants us to be. We are called to be example setters for others. The power of the Word of God through us is able to transform lives and change all situations.

What we have been given is not like a new purse or a new car. It is not something that can get old and need to be replaced. What we have been given is eternal. Isaiah 40:8 says it like this, "*the grass withers and flowers fade, but the word of our God shall stand forever.*" It will never wear out, we do not need to replace it and there is no substitute for it.

It is up to us to receive this gift. Just because it has been given to you, does not mean that you have received it. How do we receive the gift we have been given? Romans 10:17 says that "*faith comes by hearing and hearing by the Word of God.*" Notice that scripture does not say faith comes by having heard the Word of God. No, this is present tense that means that we must hear the Word regularly, over and over again so that faith can come to us. Without hearing the Word, we cannot grow in faith. If we do not hear the Word, the gift we have been given is non effective in our lives, it is like a Christmas gift that never gets used. You know that sweater that your in-laws gave you that just sat in the closet and got holes in it, or that knick-knack that your aunt gave you that sat in the curio cabinet and collected dust. We get no use out of it and it means really nothing in our lives. THAT IS NOT THE INTENT OF THE GIFT OF THE WORD OF GOD.

The Word that has been given to us is special, it is able to create something new for us if we receive it and use it.

As a woman, you have many things and people that pull you in all kinds of ways. I pray that this book will encourage you to stay strong and recognize that God's infinite power is able to help you overcome every challenge and every obstacle that you face.

As you read this book I encourage you to dust off your Bible, open it up and allow the Spirit of God to lead you in reading and studying the Word. Read out loud to yourself, remember the Scripture, "faith comes by HEARING, and hearing by the Word of God (Romans 10:17). You must hear the Word in order for faith to come.

Also, keep a notebook with you to write down the many things you hear in the Spirit. Watch over time how every prayer, every misunderstanding and every question you have gets answered or corrected by the Word of God!

So I say to you... Be Encouraged!

Week 1: Woman Where Are You?

A woman should be so hidden in Christ that only a man seeking God can find her. – Maya Angelou

I saw this quote in an email that I received. This statement is so, so, true. It is fitting if you are married, single (praying for a husband), single (not praying for a husband), divorced (desiring a husband or if you are not interested in a husband), whatever your situation.

Think about what this says: We as women should be wrapped up in Christ, so that we are concealed, out of sight and not readily apparent to anyone unless they are seeking God. Matthew 6:33 says, "Seek ye **first** the kingdom of God and His righteousness, and all these things shall be added unto you." *Seeking the kingdom of God is our way of hiding* in Christ. We become so involved with the Word of God and getting wisdom and understanding of the Word, that we cannot be understood or likened to the World around us, as a result people not seeking God see us as strange and "out there", whereas people (men) seeking God, see us as God sees us, as beautiful women of God.

I am reminded of the lyrics to a song by Clint Brown that says:

Just to be close to you, is where I long to be
Let me hide myself inside your heart to find my destiny
Every step I take, is one less step I'll need
To be in your presence and close to thee

Hiding in Christ is worshiping him. It is us demonstrating to God that He is who we need; who we long to be with, it is telling Him that You are worthy, You are worth my time, my praise, and my adoration. A truth is, we love our spouses our children and our friends, but no love is greater than the love between you and God. Our love to our spouses and children is an extension of our love with God. Without the love between you and God as a foundation, you are not even able to love other people.

Hiding in Christ puts you face to face with God. You cannot hide from God!!!! He sees you as who you are, faults, disappointments, failures, etc. But although He sees you, He sees an opportunity to correct the things that are not right in you. It is like a piece of gold being purified. If you take the raw gold and place it in a furnace and turn up the heat, all the impurities will fall off, leaving a piece of pure refined gold. Sometimes, when the gold comes out, the luster is still not right, there are still some superficial impurities left, so it has to go back into the furnace and be reheated, and then brought out again. That furnace is like our hiding in Christ. That is where God is removing all the impurities and superficial attachments in our hearts, we are being purified.

We must hide in Christ all the time, because everyday something of the world tries to attach itself to us and sometimes, we attach ourselves to the world. James 4:8 says, *"Draw nigh to God, and He will draw nigh to you. Cleanse your hands, ye sinners; and purify your hearts, ye double minded."* God desires a real relationship with you, one where He takes His Holy Word and speaks life to you. He takes His Word and comforts you, He takes His Word and guides and directs your steps, He takes His Word and prospers you, He takes His Word and answers all of your questions, and He takes His Word and transforms your mind into the mind of Christ. By His Word, your whole life can be changed and made new.

Action Step for the Week:

Meditate on scriptures that will transform and renew your mind. Say them out loud so you can put voice to the Word of God. Once you speak His Word out of your mouth, expect what you say to happen.

Isaiah 55:11 says, *"so shall my word be that goes forth out of my mouth: it shall not return unto me void, but it shall accomplish that which I please, and it shall prosper in the thing whereto I sent it."* You are giving voice to the Word of God; this scripture says that it will accomplish what it was sent to do!

Week 2: Master Your Emotions

This week's encouragement is to help us align our emotions with the will and Word of God. Proverbs 3:5, 6 says, "*trust in the Lord with all your heart and lean not unto your own understanding. In all of your ways acknowledge Him and He will direct your path*". Our lives should be lead by the Spirit of God and not by our emotions.

Women by nature are emotional beings. We are the nurturer of our families; we comfort our children and spouses. We are a shoulder for a friend in need; we pray with those in turmoil, we rejoice when something good happens to our co-workers. We are reservoirs of emotion. All too often, we allow our emotions to get us into trouble. We often make decisions based on emotions. This can be very dangerous especially when the decisions that are being made are major life changing decisions. When we allow our emotions to dictate our decisions, we are operating in the flesh and not in the Spirit (1 Corinthians 3:1)

Humans are three part beings. We have a spirit, a soul and a body. Each part has a specific purpose, for example, the body is the housing for the spirit and the soul, the spirit (our heart) is the part of us that is connected to God and the soul is a combination of our mind, will and emotions.

If we analyze the soul, we will find that it is the part of us that makes decisions, suggestions, has ideas, it is the place where meditation occurs, we think pleasant and unpleasant thoughts, we dream, fantasize, daydream, we feel... like crying, laughing, we feel pain, anger, happiness, disappointment, and the like. It is the hub that connects us to fleshly things of this world. Without the soul we would not be able to have a free will or even make our own decisions. God has given us the ability to choose.

Our emotions are not meant to be used to guide our decision making, but rather to be like a barometer. A barometer measures the atmosphere's pressure; from this reading a prediction can be made for the next day's weather. For example, will it be warm, rainy or snowing. This pressure alone cannot determine a weather report, but this pressure with other factors helps to predict a complete weather report. The same is true for our emotions. If something terrible happens and we experience the feeling of sadness, this alone is no indicator of what our day or our response to people should be; but rather a check point for ourselves to determine the next step we should take according to the Word of God.

If your emotions are not put into check they will lead you down a dangerous and perhaps deadly path. Take Eve for example; in the Garden of Eden, she decided to allow her emotions to lead her to spiritual death. Genesis 3:6 says, *"And when the woman saw that the tree was good for food, and that it was pleasant to the eyes, and a tree to be desired to make one wise, she took of the fruit thereof, and did eat..."* Eve's emotions were working overtime here, she saw the fruit look "Good" and that she would be wise. She wanted it, so she took and ate the forbidden food. She did not take into account what God had said about her dying as a result of eating this fruit. She allowed her emotions to determine her thinking and thus her decision making.

The same is true for us, how many times did we purchase something item that we knew would mess up our budget? What about the countless times you gave someone a piece of your mind because you did not like what they said to you? What about the number of times you decided to disobey the Word of God because you felt like doing your own thing? These examples show up in our lives when we decide to be lead by our flesh and emotions and not by the Spirit of God.

Unchecked emotions move us out of submission to God and out of His will for our lives. We must take authority over our emotions and bring them into subjection to the will of God so that we can make godly decisions for our lives. 2 Corinthians 10:5, commands us to cast down everything that tries to exalt itself above the Word of God, and bring into subjection every thought to the obedience of God.

Action Steps for this Week:

Check out your emotions this week. See if they line up with the Word of God. Are you allowing the way that you feel about something or someone control the way you respond to situations or people? Challenge yourself to line up the way you feel (your emotions) with the Word of God and then do what the Bible says versus what your feelings say.

Week 3: You Can Do Anything

Have you ever wondered how you actually do some of the things that you do? Have you ever gotten a job or a project assigned to you and you were not real sure how you would do it, because quite frankly, you did not have a clue as to what you were doing? But by the end of the project it turned out perfectly! And the job became a piece of cake! Have you sensed that God has called you to do some things that you would have never imagined that you would do, you think to yourself, sure that may be something for someone else, but not for me!

Last week a friend and I were talking about what we would do with 100 million dollars. We said we would give 25% as tithe and offering to the church, then we would open up a home for people that have overcome drugs and alcohol. We would establish a school for children ages preschool to 12; we would have transitional housing units for people that need financial, housing and life skills assistance. We would use the money to establish a variety of other services and resources. If God would put the money in our hands we would continue to build the kingdom of God through these programs.

God quickly lead me to Philippians 4:13, *"I can do all things through Christ which strengthens me."* All I need is faith in God and all things are possible (Matthew 19:26). Through Christ I can do this, but it has to be in and through Him only. I cannot look at the situation and say, oh, I do not have the money, we have no buildings or houses, and we lack resources. No, I must say what I expect to see, that is what it means to operate in faith. So my confession has changed to, thank you Lord for putting in my hands all the resources needed to build your kingdom on this earth, there is no lack because you supply all my needs according to your riches in glory by Christ Jesus (Philippians 4:19). My job is to trust God and know that He will do what He said!

How is it that some things we set out to do come to fruition but many others fail? The answer is simple; we are not operating through Christ, but through our own abilities. Proverbs 3:5, 6 says, *"Trust in the Lord with all your heart and lean not to your own understanding, in all your ways acknowledge Him and He will direct your path."* Even if you are a single parent or a married parent that feels that they are doing everything alone. God is with you, He is there for you. He is giving you the strength that you need to complete every task and assignment, but you must trust Him. God already knows exactly what He wants for your life. You do not have to figure anything out. Yes, it seems hard sometimes as if you are in this thing called life alone, but the truth is, it only seems that way, because you are putting your trust in your own abilities and not solely relying on God.

The Word trust means to rely and depend on. Yes, we work jobs so that we can earn money to pay our bills, but our jobs are not our source. GOD is our SOURCE, without Him we would not have a job or the ability to perform the job. In His divine plan for your life He has already mapped out what He wants for you. Jeremiah 1:5 (paraphrased) says *"I knew you before you were formed in your mother's womb. I called you, I ordained you."* He knows your inner most feelings, you hurts, your desires, He knows exactly what you like and dislike. He continues in Jeremiah 29:11 to say, *"For I know the thoughts that I think toward you, says the LORD, thoughts of peace, and not of evil, to prosper you and not to harm you."* God wants to prosper you in every area of your life, your health, your family, your finances, your relationships, your service at church, your ability to give to others, everything that you do He wants to prosper, but it is only through and by HIM that it will happen.

Action Steps for this Week:

This week focus on trusting in the Lord. It is painful and often times agonizing to try to figure in your mind how bills will get paid, how you will work, pick up the kids, cook dinner, go to basketball practice, give the kids a bath and all the other many things you must do in a day. Why not try God! Let Him dictate your day and allow Him to decide when and how things will happen, seek Him before making plans for the day and see if He does not order your day so that you will have peace that passes all understanding (Phil 4:7)!

Week 4: You Are Forgiven

This week's encouragement is to help us understand that we are forgiven by God for all of our sins!

How many times in your life have you had to decide to either sin or operate in the truth of the Word of God? You do have the choice to sin or obey the Word of God. Sin does not just happen, it is a choice that we make when faced with a situation. (Romans 6:1-23)

Many people think that sin is something only "bad" people do, you know, the ones that don't go to church or believe in God. But the Bible says that all of us have sinned, even those who believe in God (Romans 3:23).

Did you know that sin is as simple as not obeying God when you hear His voice, or not assembling with believers when they gather (Hebrews 10:25). Sin is thinking those lustful and ungodly thoughts about that handsome man that you saw at the mall, and in your mind you went to places you should not have (Matthew 5:28 – yes, this scripture applies to women looking at men). Sin is telling only a part of a truth, which is really a lie (Colossians 3:9).

Sin is being jealous of your friend who got that promotion that you really wanted, outside you appear happy for her, but inside you are green with envy. Sin is often hating those around you, because you do not like what they do (Titus 3:3). Sin is not obeying your husband when he has told you not to do a certain thing and you decide, I am my own woman, I can do what I want! (Ephesians 5:22) Sin is not trusting that the Word will do what it says that it will do (Isaiah 55:11). And the list goes on and on.

Sins that get captured by the media are the ones we normally consider as "real sins", murder, adultery, fornication, stealing, lying, and so on. But the scripture says that it is the small foxes that spoil the vine (Song of Solomon 2:15). That means it is all those little things that we think are insignificant that add up to make one very big problem.

Think about this statement: *Sinning wouldn't be so popular if its wages were paid immediately.* If God paid us for the sins that we committed instantly, this earth would be void of people as the Bible says that the wages of sin is death (Romans 6:23). But thanks be to God for Jesus Christ that He died for our sins and has given us the ability to repent and be forgiven.

Daily, I repent for my sins both known and unknown; those things that I did, knowing that God would not want me to have done them as they go against His Word, and those things that I did not realizing that I did them. God is faithful and just to forgive us of all of our sins!

That means we no longer need to feel shameful and feel guilty about what we did in the past, but we can stand boldly before God because of Jesus Christ! 1 John 1:9 says *"if we confess our sins, He is faithful and just to forgive us our sins, and to cleanse us from all unrighteousness."* This is good news, whatever the sin was we can confess it and we are forgiven right now. We can walk with our heads up high knowing that Christ has made us clean through His blood. Hebrews 8:10 says, *"I will be merciful to their unrighteousness, and their sins and their iniquities will I remember no more."*

If God has forgiven you and forgotten about your past sins, why haven't you? You are a child of the King, He loves you, He has forgiven you and He wants you to forgive yourself and move on so that your life can prosper!

Action Steps for this week:

1. Daily ask God to forgive your sins.
2. Before making choices ask yourself is this what God would want me to do or will this be a sin?
3. Forgive yourself and remember your sins no more.

Week 5: You Must Have Expectation

Do you expect great things for your life? Your expectation will determine your harvest. If you do not expect anything, nothing will happen. This week's encouragement is designed to get you expecting big things for this year. Did you know that you can dream and imagine doing anything? As a matter of fact, you actually can have what you dream about.

I asked a group of women to tell me where they would go if offered the opportunity to travel anywhere in the world and money and time were of no concern. Sadly, most of the answers were, I do not know or I do not like to travel; some said maybe California. Just think, you can go anywhere; why not imagine yourself on an island in Bermuda, or even walking the streets of Paris. Most of these women could not imagine themselves outside of the state of Minnesota. Their expectation for life was very limited, so much so, that they were afraid to think outside of the small box that they had created for themselves.

I want you to open your mind and see yourself outside of your present circumstances. See yourself as who you desire to be and not who you are right now. Take a moment and visualize this, now take a picture. Post that picture in your mind. Set your expectation on seeing yourself doing and being something great. The Bible says that our expectation should come from the Lord (Psalm 62:5). God knows our beginning and our end and He says that our end is much greater than our beginning (Job 8:7). That means that we are destined for something great. You could be the next great inventor or Noble Prize winner.

Because you belong to God, you have an advantage, an upper hand on life. You have favor and the blessing of the Lord. Every day is a new opportunity for you to do something great. Today you are one step closer to your destiny and because of that you should be looking for great things to happen just for you.

Action Steps for This Week:

This week I encourage you to actually see yourself doing something great. Perhaps you see yourself as the president of a company, owning a prosperous business, becoming a millionaire, inventing a new product; the sky is the limit and you have the power and ability to do anything!

Write down your outside of the box ideas. Take an action step by researching one of your ideas to find out what it would take to put into motion your idea.

Week 6: You Must Be Humble

Have you heard the phrase, "Life is not fair", perhaps from your children when they do not get their way? I remember a time when I told my daughter, when she used this phrase, I told her that she was right, life is not fair, but we serve a just and loving God.

As an adult we often see life very differently than children. They see things as very simple as we see them as complex. Children see themselves getting what they want as how things should be whereas we as adults see getting what we want as difficult tasks. What if everything that we wanted out of life was right at our fingertips! What if all the hopes and dreams that we have in our hearts have already been promised to us and all we have to do is open the right door and walk in and live! Wouldn't that be exciting?

The Bible teaches us that unless we come to God as a child (humble) we cannot enter the kingdom of God (God's way of doing things) Mark 10:15. God's kingdom is the way that He does His business. That means that whatever the Bible says is what He is going to do, He will not change His way of doing things according to Malachi 3:6 and Hebrews 13:8.

In order for God to fulfill the promises that He has for you, you have to see yourself the way that God sees you, as "HUMBLE". We must put ourselves below God and allow Him to govern us. In doing so, we can receive the fulfillment of all of His promises.

It is your right as a child of God to have all of these things operating in your life:

1. Health – 3 John 2
2. Financial Security – Joshua 1:8
3. Peace – Galatians 5:22, Philippians 4:7
4. Joy – Romans 14:17
5. Empowered to be a blessing to someone else – Genesis 12:2, 3
6. Faith to move mountains – Matthew 17:20

And many more, the Bible is full of the promises that God has just for you. They are right at your fingertips!!!

In order to receive them, you have to first humble yourself. Then you have to let God be God in your life. Yes, there are some things that God asks us to do as His children, but what parent does not have requirements of their children? These requirements are not hard, they are simple; to love me, put no one before me and keep my commandments (Mark 12:30 and John 14:15).

Action Steps for this Week:

1. I challenge you this week to really focus on humbling yourself. Put your desires and wants behind those of God. Put your spouse and children first, consider their wants.
2. Find 10 promises in the Bible that God has for you. Meditate on them and then allow God to manifest them in your life!

Week 7: Don't Give Up

My husband wrote a song a few years back called, *Don't Give Up*. Its lyrics describe how he grew up in a dead end situation, a life with no parents around, struggling to find food and shelter, and living a life that was going no where. But, he always knew God and that God would bring Him out if he did not give up.

Hearing that song and understanding the magnitude of what he experienced makes me recognize that I lived a very different life than him. Although different, we still had the commonality of needing to depend on God. All of us face situations that put us into a position to want to give up. People talk a lot about obstacles that they face as well as stumbling blocks put in their way by people that are close to them.

You encounter a many people in life. For example there is the group that wants you to succeed, but really does nothing to help you get to success. Then there is the group that would rather see you doing nothing to better yourself, they want you to stay just like them, STUCK IN A RUT, and they tell you that nothing will work for you because nothing has worked for them.

Listen to me; do not stop doing what God has purposed in your heart even though it may look like you are going no where. The Bible says that God has purposed your life for something. Jeremiah 29:11 says, *"For I know the thoughts that I think toward you, says the LORD, thoughts of peace, and not of evil, to give you an expected end."* That sounds to me like **God has something special just for you**. From the time that you were born you were created to do something great. That greatness does not come to fruition by sitting around waiting for something to happen. No, it comes when you put one foot in front of the other and begin walking out the plan that God has for your life. You will not start walking or even continue to walk if there are stumbling blocks in your path way. Stumbling blocks are people and situations that show up in your life to deter you from continuing on your journey.

A parent that is fearful of failure may be a stumbling block. A confidant or co-worker afraid to try something new can be a stumbling block. A best friend that is envious of your new career path may be a stumbling block. Lack of money, lack of confidence, and lack of perseverance are stumbling blocks. These things and people try to stop you from accomplishing specific tasks that you know in your heart you are supposed to do.

Every time a situation or someone rises up to tell you what you cannot do and how hard something is, you remember Jesus and the Cross. Jesus endured beating, being spit on, He endured ridicule and even death upon the cross so that you would have no reason to fear failure or defeat.

Action Step for this Week:
Make this your confession and stand firm on this foundational scripture, regardless of your situation no matter how bad it is know that God will bring you through it! Every time a doubter comes along or you begin to feel like giving up, say these words out loud!

Isaiah 50:4-9, "*The Lord GOD hath given me the tongue of the learned, that I should know how to speak a word in season to Him that is weary: He wakes me morning by morning, He opens mine ear to hear as the learned. The Lord GOD hath opened mine ear, and I was not rebellious, neither turned away back. I gave my back to the smiters, and my cheeks to them that plucked off the hair: I hid not my face from shame and spitting. For the Lord GOD will help me; therefore shall I not be confounded: therefore have I set my face like a flint, and I know that I shall not be ashamed. He is near that justifies me; who will contend with me? Let us stand together: who is mine adversary? Let Him come near to me. Behold, the Lord GOD will help me; who is he that shall condemn me? Lo, they all shall wax old as a garment; the moth shall eat them up.*"

You possess strength, power, and ability on the inside. Take that power, strength and ability and use it to do all that God has purposed in your life, Don't Give Up!

Week 8: Run Your Race

I want you to know that you can have a happy, successful and wonderful life. You can finish your race!

Ecclesiastes 9:11 states that "*the race is not given to the swift nor the battle to the strong, but to the one that endures until the end.*" The Apostle Paul writes in 1 Corinthians 9:24, 25 (AMP) "*that in a race all the runners compete, but [only] one receives the prize? So run [your race] that you may lay hold [of the prize] and make it yours. Now every athlete who goes into training conducts himself temperately and restricts himself in all things. They do it to win a wreath that will soon wither, but we [do it to receive a crown of eternal blessedness] that cannot wither.*"

If you think about a marathon, say a 5K race that is a great distance that one must travel by foot, some runners are strong and will finish the race first, others not so strong and still others may be novices and pretty weak and more than likely will come in last. We can compare our lives to being in a race. Each of us has a beginning and an end to our race. Each of us has hurdles we must overcome. During our race we may get tired and winded. Nevertheless, we have a common goal, finishing our race.

In order to finish our race we have to understand some very important facts. First, we are not in competition with anyone. Unlike a marathon that has competitors that are competing for the first place title, we have no one to run against; we are not even racing against a clock. Second, to be successful in completing our race we have to stay in "training". We have to allow God to continuously feed us spiritual food (the Word of God) so that we have the perseverance, faith and strength to complete our race. Third, unlike a marathon your prize is not tangible, it is not a gold cup or blue ribbon, or millions of dollars, your prize is fulfilling you purpose and destiny for the life that God has given to you.

You have a unique race designed for only you. God knows how He wants to get you from point A to point Z. Therefore, in your race you may experience some things that your best friend may not have to experience. You may receive blessings that your friends do not receive. That does not make you more special than anyone else, but rather these are the things that God needs you to experience so that you can grow in faith to accomplish <u>your</u> purpose and attain <u>your</u> destiny for life. When we do not understand what God's plan is for our lives, we complain about our circumstances and we question God's motives and intents for our lives. All the while, God is watching over us, guiding us and pushing us closer and closer to finishing our race.

<u>Action Step for this Week:</u>

1. Eliminate complaining and questioning God about your life. Start seeing each circumstance that you face as stepping stones to your divine purpose for life.

2. Embrace your life; it is the only one that you are going to get! Allow God to show you how to make adjustments to make your life what He wants it to be. God only wants the best for you and He will surely guide you in the right direction.

Stay strong and be encouraged, you will finish.

Week 9: God's Place in Your Life

Did you know that God is committed to helping you, loving you and meeting your needs? In the same way, we have to be committed to putting God in His rightful place. We have to prioritize God. What place does He hold in your life? Is He second, third or fourth? Or do you have Him as your number one, first place in your life. Priorities are determined by what is important to you as an individual. No one can dictate what you will do day to day except for you. My tasks this week is to encourage you to think about where God is in your life and then if necessary, help you make some adjustments, to move Him into His rightful place.

For Lazarus and his family, God was #1, it was Lazarus' sister Mary that had washed Jesus feet and dried them with her hair and then anointed Him with the costly perfume. It was the same Mary and Martha that served Jesus and the disciples an abundant feast. They had already demonstrated that God was their priority. But then a tragic situation occurred. Word came that Lazarus was sick. Jesus was asked to come so that he could be healed. But Jesus decided not to go just yet. Nevertheless, Lazarus died, leaving a family in bitter turmoil, not understanding why Jesus the Christ, the one that they knew could heal, did not come and perform a miracle for them. He did it for others why not them?

Jesus priority at that time was not to go when the family asked, because something greater than healing was to take place for this family. Sure, everyone knew that Jesus could heal Lazarus, just as He had healed those who were sick, blind, deaf and those who could not speak.

POINT #1 -Just because God does not do what you think He should do nor do something according to your time schedule, does not mean that He has forgotten about you.

God's infinite wisdom makes Him able to know what to do for you even when you cannot see it. This family knew what they had seen.

Martha knew about the resurrection of the dead in the last days, but she had not quite understood that Jesus was the resurrection. She did not quite understand that He was able to resurrect her brother.

POINT #2 –Don't discount God just because you have not seen or experienced all of His power operating in your life!

The story of Lazarus ends when Jesus resurrects Him from the dead; Jesus actually calls Him out of the grave. His exact words were, *"Lazarus, come forth."* From this ending we see that God's plan for Lazarus and this family was more than just healing. God had a resurrection for Lazarus in store all along. (John 11:1-44).

Action Steps for this Week:

1. Read John 11:1-44 the complete story of Lazarus and his resurrection.
2. Identify the areas of your life need to be resurrected (brought back to life). Is it your relationship with God? Your marriage? Your relationship with your family?
2. Allow God through the power of His Word to resurrect each area of your life that you have identified.

Week 10: Completing Your Journey

On your journey to fulfilling your destiny you will encounter many things, some good and some not so good. Sometimes it seems like you have reached a fork in the road. Down one side you see what things and people that will help you on this road, your familiar past. But down the other side appears to be the unknown, people you do not know and situations that you have never encountered before. So you find yourself taking the path filled with things and people that you are familiar, needless to say you have taken the wrong path. You find yourself distracted from God's perfect plan, you are worried, you are uneasy about everything and furthermore, you find yourself going back to the things that God has freed you from. You keep encountering the same old situations with the same old people and frankly, you are just tired of all of it!

If you want new results you are going to have to do some things you have never done before. The first step is going back to that fork in the road and choosing the other path. This path is filled with fresh experiences that will strengthen you and grow you up into a strong and powerful woman. But, if you refuse to go through these new experiences you will not gain the benefits of the wisdom and knowledge that come with them. Some of these experiences are painful and uncomfortable at the time, but after the sting is gone, you can look back and say, I learned so much and my life has increased. God has a way of purifying us on this road with His Word. That purification is removing all the toxins that have attached themselves to us, those things that are in our innermost being that only He can pull out.

If you think about Jesus, when He left glory to come to earth to save us, He knew that He was going to have to be beaten, jailed and hung on the cross, yet He endured till the end, because it was His destiny. It was not for Him, but for all of us. In the same way, your life is not for you, but for those that you deal with on a daily basis and all of those that will come after you. The mark that you make is a treasure for someone else.

Completing your journey is required not optional. Therefore, I encourage you today to dust yourself off. Hold your head up high and thank the Lord that you have another opportunity to go back to that fork in the road and try again! Sure, you may have been weak these past few days or weeks or even years, but right now today, you are starting over where you left off. The Scripture says that Jesus finished His race and so can we. We have to keep our eyes on the finish line and recharge ourselves with the Word of God.

Action Step for this Week:

1. Dust yourself off and get back on the road to your destiny.

2. Whenever you begin to get weak and think it is getting to hard, read this scripture and make it your motivation to keep going:

Hebrews 12:1-3 (Message Bible)

"Do you see what this means—all these pioneers who blazed the way, all these veterans cheering us on? It means we'd better get on with it. Strip down, start running—and never quit! No extra spiritual fat, no parasitic sins. Keep your eyes on Jesus, who both began and finished this race we're in. Study how he did it. Because He never lost sight of where He was headed—that exhilarating finish in and with God—He could put up with anything along the way: cross, shame, whatever. And now He's there, in the place of honor, right alongside God. When you find yourselves flagging in your faith, go over that story again, item by item, that long litany of hostility He plowed through. That will shoot adrenaline into your souls!"

Week 11: Your Challenges are Opportunities for Growth

If your last week was a challenging one, join the club. Many of us encountered major road blocks, obstacles and difficult decisions that had to be made. If you felt anything like me, you were stressed and completely drained, looking for a serious vacation!

Stay strong! Joshua 1:6 says, *"Be strong and courageous."* This life that we live in comes with many surprises and unexpected issues that seem unbearable at the time. You probably asked yourself, "Why do I have to deal with this? Surely, I do not deserve what I am getting!"

Everything in life that comes to our doorstep is not always "deserved" or even asked for. In life things come at us for two main reasons. One is the principle of seedtime and harvest. What you sow is what you will reap (Gal 6:7). Did you sow bad seeds that have generated a bad harvest? We have to make sure that in every situation we understand that whatever we decide will come back on us whether good or bad. Therefore, make sure that what you say and do unto others is what you want to come back to you.

The second reason things happen to us is because this life that we live comes with trials and tribulations, but we are told in James 1:2, 3, *"to count it all joy when ye fall into divers temptations or trials; Knowing this, that the trying of your faith works patience."* We do not always have a say in what we deal with from day to day, but we can control how we handle each situation. You can decide that the trials that you face will NOT get the best of you. But rather you will increase in patience as a result of the situation. Moreover, whatever it is you face, you use it to become a stronger and wiser person. The next time a circumstance like it comes along, you will already have the wisdom to deal with it.

My encouragement to you is simply this, do not despise the uncomfortable and challenging issues that you face, instead begin to use them for your advantage. Allow each situation to be a teaching tool that you can glean knowledge, wisdom and understanding. You then establish an arsenal of strength and wisdom to combat future situations that may arise in your life.

Action Step for this Week:

1. Check out the types of seeds that you are sowing through words and actions. Make sure that you are sowing words and actions that you want to harvest in your life.

2. Look at challenges, problems and issues that arise as opportunities for growth. Write down key nuggets of wisdom and knowledge that you glean from each situation.

3. Remember that each day you are getting stronger, wiser and more powerful!

Week 12: All Your Wounds Can be Healed

As we go through life we encounter various situations. Some situations bring hurt and pain leaving us with wounds and bruises in our spirits (hearts). It is not God's plan for you to live life broken and wounded. Yes, things happen and do not feel real good and may sometimes even throw us off track, but God says that *"He came to preach the gospel to the poor; He came to heal the brokenhearted, to preach deliverance to the captives, and recovering of sight to the blind, to set at liberty them that are bruised, To preach the acceptable year of the Lord."* (Luke 4:18).

Most people never deal with the source of the wounds that they carry. They cover them with a band-aid. On the inside they are confused, miserable and full of anger and bitterness. So in order to cope with their problems, they turn their focus onto something that takes the focus away from the real issue. In order to become a completely healed person, each of those wounds has to be uncovered and healed from the inside out.

Have you gotten to the point that you are tired of hanging onto hatred, anger, strife and bitterness between you and other people? Wouldn't life be so much easier if you could simply forgive yourself for that thing you did years past that keeps haunting you? What about those relationships that have been broken due to betrayal and dishonesty? God has a plan to take care of all of these things, but you have to be willing to let go of all of it.

God is ready and willing to heal your broken heart, forgive you of your past, and start you fresh and new, but you have to decide to leave every piece of baggage at His feet. 1 Peter 5:7 *says "Cast your cares on Him for He cares for you."* God wants you to exchange your problems, anxieties, worry and every pain for His joy. Daryl Evans wrote a song that says:

I'm trading my sorrows
I'm trading my shame

I'm laying them down for the joy of the Lord
I'm trading my sickness
I'm trading my pain
I'm laying them down for the joy of the Lord

Why not trade all your pain, shame, sickness and sorrow for God's joy?

Action Steps for this Week:

This is your time to be completely healed and forgiven of all the past and healed of any wounds that you have. Trade all of the sorrow and shame for God's joy. Your job is to acknowledge the wounds and release them, God will do the rest.

1. Talk about it and leave it with God – Go into that secret place with God and acknowledge the wounds that you have.
2. Ask God to heal you from whatever it is.
3. Receive God's healing. Once you ask God to heal you, know that He has done it.
4. Meditate on scriptures about being healed whenever those old feelings rise up.
5. See yourself as an overcomer – Recognize that you are no longer that wounded person walking around hurt, but you are made new and are whole and complete in God.

Week 13: Live Everyday Stress Free

Have you heard that laughter is good medicine? In Ecclesiastes 3:4, King Solomon said, "*There is a time to weep, and a time to laugh; a time to mourn, and a time to dance.*" Laughing does have a place in our lives! Did you know that when you laugh your body releases pleasure chemicals called endorphins, the same chemicals that are released when you exercise?

In our busy lives of work, family, school, church and everything else, we often become stressed out. The pressure of performing at work, making it meetings on time, finding time to spend with your family, worrying about money and how to pay bills, concerns about your in-laws and your husband's needs. By the end of the day our bodies are stressed. When stress comes upon our bodies it releases two chemicals, adrenalin and cortisol both which can be harmful to our health and make us age faster than we should.

Laughter on the other hand blocks the harmful effects of the two stress hormones. A good session of laughing is equivalent to an aerobic work out. Laughter produces nitric oxide which allows the blood vessels to expand which is good for our cardiovascular systems and helps to reduce blood pressure. I think that it would be safe to say that laughter is Good Medicine.

I remember going to a camp meeting some years back. Kenneth Hagin was teaching. All of a sudden, the spirit of laughter broke out. It was on me and I could not stop laughing. I laughed until I cried. After the meeting was over that night, I felt so refreshed and energized. I decided that night to take laughing to a new level.

When you are faced with obstacles and you know that things are out of your control. STOP what you are doing and just laugh. People may look at you funny, but realize that you are releasing stress from your life! Don't allow the stress of any situation to over take you, but rather take control by laughing out loud, until you feel a release. This may sound really simple, but it is an awesome way to stay balanced.

Action Steps for this Week:

Laugh, laugh, and laugh some more…

Take the pressure and the stress of life off of your shoulders by enjoying a comedy, reading a funny book (I recommend Jesse Duplantis' *Jambalaya for the Soul*), look at old home movies; spend time with a friend who makes you laugh. If nothing else, laugh in the face of the enemy, because Christ has already won the victory for you.

Keep smiling and enjoy life!

Week 14: Your life is Redeemed from Destruction

Did you know that your life is redeemed from destruction? Not only that, but you have been given great benefits because you belong to God. According to Psalm 103:1-5 we are to "*bless the LORD, O my soul: and all that is within me bless His holy name. Bless the LORD, O my soul, and forget not all His benefits: Who forgives all my iniquities; who heals all my diseases; Who redeems my life from destruction; who crowns me with loving kindness and tender mercies; Who satisfies my mouth with good things; so that my youth is renewed like the eagle's.*"

This scripture says that we are forgiven, we are healed, we are redeemed from destruction, we are recipients of His love and mercy, He gives us only good things and we are renewed. These things are key components for living a happy and successful life, but often people do not know that these are promises that God has given to us. Therefore, we should expect to be forgiven, healed and redeemed. We should settle for nothing less than what God has said in His Word about us.

Every morning when you wake up recognize that although your circumstances and life situations may not look like you want them to, you have been given a new day to shout "my life has been redeemed from destruction." It is God's desire that you walk out this life free from sin, free from disease, and free from any danger that may try to come against you. Each one of us has been assigned angels or ministering spirits (servants) who are sent out in the service [of God for the assistance] of those who are to inherit salvation (us) (Heb 1:14 Amp). These angels are responsible to hearken to the voice of God. That means that every time you declare/confess God's Word they go and do what was said. So, if I say, my life is redeemed from destruction, based on Psalm 103:4, they have to make sure that nothing hinders me from walking in that benefit.

It is important to note that these angels do not respond to our words but only the Word of God. That is why it is so vital that we only say what God says so that we ensure that we receive the blessing of His Word.

Action Steps for this Week:

1. Thank God for all of His benefits.
2. Send out the angels that are assigned to you by making confessions and declarations of the Word of God.
3. Look for God's benefits to continuously manifest in your life.

God's Word is life to us so let us walk in it and live!

Week 15: You Deserve Happiness in Your Life

One of the greatest things that we can have is happiness, a sincere feeling of being content in what we have and in who we are. Happiness however only comes from God. According to Proverbs 16:20, *"He that handles a matter wisely shall find good: and whoso trusts in the LORD, happy is he."* We have to find ourselves putting all of our trust in the Lord for our happiness.

There are people and things in our lives that can put us in a position to not be happy. Imagine, waking up one morning and you are feeling on top of the world. You have spent time with the Lord and your day is going great. Then, just after noon, you get a phone call that informs you that someone has taken all of your money out of the bank, your entire savings is gone. What do you do? Remember, you were happy before the phone call, so now after that call you have a choice to make. Will you remain content or will you decide to allow your entire attitude and demeanor to change in to something "ugly".

The choice to put your trust in God means that you trust Him with everything; even those things that happen that push us into difficult situations. Trust is total dependence or reliance on someone. If you put your entire dependence on God with this situation and not worry about it, you will be able to deal with it wisely and handle it the way God wants you to handle it. You will recognize that although you have lost something, you can be strong and remain content knowing that God is working on your behalf.

True happiness comes when the ways of this world do not move you. No amount of money, no material possessions, no person, absolutely nothing should be able to move us out of our happy place in God. When we are able to be steadfast, unmovable and always abounding in the work of the Lord (1Corinthians 15:58), we will recognize true happiness in our lives.

Action Steps for this Week:

1. Focus on trusting God with everything.

2. Challenge yourself to not be moved by things that happen in your life each day.

3. Be happy knowing that God is on your side.

Keep the faith and be happy!

Week 16: Simplify

Have you gotten to the point that you are overwhelmed with stuff, life and people? Have you found that you cannot focus due to the high demand of your multiple jobs (family, work, church, and everything else)? Are you tired of being tired? I have a solution for all of this!

SIMPLIFY!

Remember in school when they taught us about fractions? One major test question was to take the mixed fractions add them together and then simplify. If your math skills were up to par, this was a simple task, but if you really did not understand what a mixed fraction was or how to add two fractions together, this was a very difficult task.

The same holds true for our lives. When someone tells us to simplify our lives we really do not know how to do that. We spend so much time trying to acquire things and stuff, we want to impress people, we value what others think of us and what we have as more important than what we truly value and find important. For some reason we have in our minds that we must have the most elaborate things and, well, simple things are just not good enough. It has to be flashy and expensive or else it is just not worth having.

I am reminded of a passage of Scripture where Mary is at the feet of Jesus while Martha is busy serving. When Martha recognizes that Mary is not assisting her in the serving she questions the situation wanting to know why Mary has left her to serve alone. Jesus answered and said unto her, *"Martha, Martha, thou art careful and troubled about many things: But one thing is needful: and Mary hath chosen that good part, which shall not be taken away from her."*(Luke 10:38-42)

There is truly one needful thing, the Word of God. When it comes to simplifying our lives we have to look at what God says is important and then go from there. Getting His Word every day and having a relationship with Him is first and most important. Loving and nurturing our families and providing for them is also very important. Enjoying our lives and what we do as a career is vital.

If what you do only brings stress and sorrow, it is something that is probably clouding your judgment on a lot of things. In your home, do you have stock piles of stuff because you saw it and decided "I want it"? Or do you really need it? Most of us have clothes, shoes, handbags, furniture, household items, cars, etc that we have because we want it, not that we need it or can even use all of it over the course of our life time. Why not go through your home and loose some of this stuff. We have clutter everywhere, only because we view everything as "needful". When really most of what we have is just wanted.

Action Steps for this Week:

1. Determine what is needed versus what is only wanted in your life, choose the needful things.
2. Decide to simplify. Get rid of things that clutter your mind, clothes, shoes, magazines, old newspapers, old books, household items, etc.
3. Organize what you have, ease your mind of stress knowing where everything is.
4. Decide that what you value is up to you and not anyone else. Don't have things or do things to impress other people.

This is a big task, it may take some time to get all of this done, but you can do it.

Week 17: Slow Down Your Moving Too Fast

Have you ever had one of those days where it seemed like everyone and everything was moving in slow motion? You know, on the road every car is in your way, they are driving so slow in the fast lane, you want to push them out of the way with your car. At the checkout counter in the grocery store, the person in front of you has 10,000 items and the cashier is moving at the speed of a turtle. It takes 30 minutes for your boss to give you a 3 minute assignment. You begin to ask yourself, is everyone slow or am I moving at 100 mph? Many times we operate our lives like microwaves. We want things to happen right now. We do not want to wait for anything. We do not have the time to allow God to reveal to us what we should do unless He is going to tell us NOW. Why is that? As if we have the power over God to determine how and when things should happen in our lives.

The American society has taught us for years to do what makes us feel good, and also not do those things that don't make us feel good. In other words let your feelings (or your flesh) dictate what you do in life. This principal has gotten many of us into some serious situations that did not turn out very well. I can think of countless situations where I did not take the time to listen to the Spirit and obey the voice of God. This got me into a heap of trouble. You might as well say that I had to learn the hard way that it is better to obey than to sacrifice (1 Samuel 15:22). One thing that I have learned through all of this is patience and how to wait on the Lord.

The Bible says in James 1:3 and 4 (Amplified Version), "*Be assured and understand that the trial and proving of your faith bring out endurance and steadfastness and patience. But let endurance and steadfastness and patience have full play and do a thorough work, so that you may be perfectly and fully developed [with no defects], lacking in nothing.*"

Interestingly enough, patience is linked to trials and proving of our faith. The three examples that I gave in the beginning are some things that test our faith on a daily basis. These are prime opportunities to exercise our faith. We can choose to handle a situation like God, or we can choose to operate like the world. If we choose the godly way, we will develop patience. If we opt for the other way, we perpetuate our lack of faith. The development of patience will ensure that we lack nothing in our lives. Exercising your faith puts God in a position to put us in the right places at the right times, putting us in the presence of the right people at the right times and making sure that we have an advantage and favor in every area of our lives.

Every time you pass one of these faith tests and develop your patience you are on a road to gain what is called experience. Romans 5:3 says, *"and not only so, but we glory in tribulations also: knowing that tribulation works patience; and patience, experience; and experience, hope."* This scripture reiterates that although you are faced with situations that may trouble you, the way that you handle them and come through them gives you something in return, patience and experience. Two things that you would have never received had you not gone through the situation.

How much better of a life would we live if we took the time to wait on the Lord? I know you need answers right now. You need to know where the finances are going to come from right now. Should you marry that man, right now? Do you leave your husband, right now? So many questions, but the truth is God has all of the answers; you have to be patient and wait on **HIM** to reveal them to you.

Action Steps for this Week:

1. Slow down everything!

2. Whatever situation you find yourself in, count it all JOY!

3. Seek God for what He wants you to do in that situation.

4. Listen for God's voice to know what to do.

5. Be content know that once you come through this situation, you will have gained patience and experience.

Week 18: Rest for You Soul...

Corporate types have made the term R&R very popular. After a long hard week at the office a well needed weekend retreat is in store for these hard core business people. Average everyday working people often bypass R&R due to financial situations, time constraints or children. As a result we operate our lives at less than 100% because we are run down and have not had an opportunity to recharge our batteries. In our efforts to serve people and do what God has put in us to do, we can become over burdened and forget that we need rest and relaxation too.

I remember hearing the term R&R and had no clue what that even meant, for a long time I thought it had some thing to do with the railroad system. Once I began working in the corporate arena I quickly learned that R&R is rest and relaxation. In my mind rest meant going to bed at a decent hour each night and relaxation was not being tense when you got ready to do something important. Oh how wrong I was. I experienced my most memorable R&R opportunity in August of 2005. I was so stressed out that my neck, shoulders and back were totally locked up to the point that I had a constant headache. My doctor said to me, "You need a vacation!" So, my husband and I packed a bag, bought a bunch of snacks, and water and left the kids with a family member. We found this great spot in Northern Minnesota right on the lake. The room was very tranquil and serene, I finally understood R&R. I could focus on God and not feel compelled to do a project or answer a phone.

In order for you to complete all the things that God has for you to do, you are going to need some time to recharge. I encourage you to plan regular R&R time for yourself. Your body and mind can only take so much. You can wear yourself down to the point that you are no good to yourself or those that you have to serve. Have you ever gone somewhere and the people that greet you are snappy? The people that are supposed to be friendly are short and actually rude to everyone? They simply need some time off from everything. The same is true for us. We treat people differently when we need rest. Our attitude is better when we are been refreshed. Moreover, we can better hear what God is telling us to do with our lives when we are well rested and relaxed.

There are all different types of vacations that you can take, some more expensive than others. For example: taking a trip to another country or city, a long drive to a Bed and Breakfast, a retreat center, or one of my favorites, an all day spa.

You can easily do a one day vacation by taking the kids to school, if you are married, perhaps your husband will be at work, you can take the day off. Go to the gym and get a great sweat, shower up and then go to the spa ask for a full body massage, get a pedicure and/or manicure or even try a facial, better yet get it all. After your spa treatments get a great salad and spend the last hour or two reading your favorite magazine, praying or reading the Bible, you even have time for a nap. Not only will you feel better about yourself, you will have more energy and it is great for your skin and your spirit!

Jesus says in Matthew 11:28 (Message Bible), *"Are you tired? Worn out? Burned out on religion? Come to me. Get away with me and you'll recover your life. I'll show you how to take a real rest. Walk with me and work with me—watch how I do it. Learn the unforced rhythms of grace. I won't lay anything heavy or ill-fitting on you. Keep company with me and you'll learn to live freely and lightly."* God wants to give you "His" rest. While you spend time resting and relaxing, you can allow your mind and spirit to open up to God and allow Him to give you true rest.

Action Steps for this Week:

1. Plan a monthly, quarterly or semi annual vacation.
2. Treat yourself to a spa session at least once every few months.
3. Drink a cup of Chamomile tea before bed.
4. Take some time to do things that relax you each day.

Week 19: God's Grace is Sufficient for You

The word grace means unmerited favor, it means a temporary exemption, and it is a virtue extended to us from God. When God sent Jesus to die for our sins He extended to us something that we can never pay for salvation. Often people ask, "Why did He do it?" John 3:16 says, "*For God so loved the world that He gave His only begotten son, so that whosoever believes in Him will have life and have life more abundantly.*" So, we can surmise that Jesus died for us because He loves us and wants us to have abundant life.

Because of Adam's (the first man) trespass, sin entered the world and death reigned over everyone, but all of those who receive [God's] overflowing grace (unmerited favor) and the free gift of righteousness [putting them into right standing with Himself] reign as kings in life through the one Man Jesus Christ (the Messiah, the Anointed One). God made grace available to us so that we did not have to receive the wages of sin which is death (Romans 3:23).

God's grace is given to us simply because God wants to give it to us. We cannot earn it, buy it or do things to get it (Romans 11:6). The Amplified Bible says in Romans 3:24, "*All are justified and made upright and in right standing with God, **freely** and gratuitously by His grace (His unmerited favor and mercy), through the redemption which is provided in Christ Jesus.*" That means that God gives us grace because He can, even though the wages of sin is death, God gives us the opportunity to repent so that we can live in our abundant life.

Truly God's grace is sufficient for you. "*My grace is sufficient for thee: for my strength is made perfect in weakness.*" (2 Corinthians 12:9) It does not matter where you find yourself today, whether you be dealing with hard decisions, easy ones or life or death situations, you may be at your weakest point, but God's grace is sufficient to handle whatever it is.

Actions Steps for this Week:

1. Rededicate your life to God. Ask Him again to come into your heart and cleanse you.
2. Receive His grace and righteousness for your life. Remember it is a free gift; Jesus has already paid for it.
3. Begin reigning as a king (queen) in this life through Jesus Christ and his Anointing! God's favor says you have a right to reign in this life.
4. Accept the fact that God loves you and He will never stop!

Week 20: God Loves You

The true issue is not "Does God Love Me"; the true issue is have you received the love of God.

To determine if you have received God's love you have to make sure that you are operating in three specific areas.

1. <u>Do you trust God with Everything?</u>
Have you given every area of your life over to God? Do you depend on Him for answers to all of your questions and problems? Is He your confidant? Do you allow Him to be involved in your daily to do's? Do you ask Him what to do when you don't know what to do?

Have you conquered the fear of worldly circumstances, such as money, jobs, family problems, terrorism, wars, and the like?

To know if you have received God's love you have to completely turn your life over to God. Do not hold on to any areas, otherwise, that will be an entrance into your life for the enemy.

The following scriptures will assist you in trusting God:

Psalm 18:2, 30	Psalm 56:11	Proverb 29:5
Psalm 37:4, 5	Psalm 125:1-3	Proverb 30:5

2. <u>Are you meditating on the Word and studying the Word on a regular basis?</u>
Just like we spend time with a loved one or someone we enjoy talking to, we have to do that same thing with God. You must get to know Him by spending time with Him, reading His Word, fellowshipping with other believers over His Word, meditating on His Word, and allowing God's Word to overtake everything that you do in life.

Philippians 3:4	Psalm 49:3	2 Timothy 2:15
Joshua 1:8a	Psalm 119:15, 16	1 John 2:3, 4

3. Are you doing what God has told you to do?

You know that you have received God's Love when you obey His commandments and do what He says, then and only then do you see His power operating in your life.

You must go and do what God says. God provides us with everything that we need to be successful in life, but it is up to us to take what He gives us and use it. He will not force us to do anything, but He will put something in your hand or in your heart and tell you now go and do this, but you have to make the choice to get up and go and do it.

Obey His commandments - Go and do what he said.

Deut 11:26, 27	Joshua 1:8b	Acts 5:29
Deut 28:1-13	Ps 119:17	John 14:21

It is God's desire to truly love you unconditionally, but we have to make sure that we love God back. Loving God shows Him that we have received His love. We do this when we obey His commandments John 14:21 says *"if you love me, keep my commandments."*

Action Steps for this Week:

Read and meditate on the scriptures in this chapter to build your faith and confidence in God's love for you.

Week 21: God's Standard

Living below God's standard has become a way of life for many believers. For some reason many people have made the decision to operate at a level of lack rather than in the overflow. This week's encouragement is meant to help open your eyes to God's desire for you to live in the OVERFLOW.

The Bible says that Jesus was made poor that through His poverty you might have abundance (2 Corinthians 8:9). He was not poor as we know poor. But he came down from heaven, the richest most glorious place in the universe, to the earth to live. So, He became poor by leaving heaven. Abundance is having more than enough. If you have an abundance of goods, you will have a sufficient amount for your family as well as enough for someone else.

Just enough is a phrase that many believer's use because they don't want to appear to have "too much". But, based on the scriptures, we are supposed to have more than enough so that we can be a blessing to someone else (Genesis 12:3).

One big hurdle that believer's must overcome is the poverty mentality. This is the mind set of living in lack. The poverty mentality only sees the next meal, the next clothing purchase; it only sees the short term and not the long term things in life. The poverty mentality would rather buy a $100 pair of tennis shoes for a child than use that same money to purchase something that will bring more than a temporary enjoyment. The poverty mentality always wants someone to give something to them. They are gimme, gimme, gimme people versus give, give, give people.

Living in the overflow means that you have crossed over into the principle of seedtime and harvest and have begun to live in the overflow of your harvest. Once you have operated in seedtime and harvest you have developed a momentum. Now you are accustom to doing things this way because you know this is what it takes to get a harvest. As you begin harvesting the seeds that you have sown you begin to live in abundance, that abundance puts you into the realm of the overflow. Pretty soon you have so much of what you have been sowing that you are now living in the "OVERFLOW". (Read Mark 4:3-20)

It is my sincere desire that each of you operate and live life in the overflow. No more lack!!!!! If you are a child of God, you have a right to live in the overflow. You have a right to operate in seedtime and harvest and you have a right to have an abundance of whatever you have sown, whether it be money, love, peace, longsuffering, patience, whatever.

Action Steps for This Week:

What do you need to do to move into a life of overflow? Take these steps:

1. Understand the principle of seedtime and harvest. (Mark 4:3-20 is a good place to begin). Understand what the Bible says about sowing and reaping.
2. Begin operating your life in seedtime and harvest without exceptions. That means every area of your life, you live by this principle.
3. Do not eat your seed. If you need more money, you must begin to sow that money and give it where God says give it. As you begin to reap a harvest of that seed, continue to sow it until you have an abundance of it, do not eat it.
4. See yourself living from your harvest. That is, the money that you reap as a result of giving. The money that you make on your job is not harvest money, it is seed.

It may not happen overnight, but truly the Word of God cannot return void. It will accomplish what is says!

Week 22: An Ordered Life

Spring is a wonderful time of year. Every year it seems that I feel a sense of newness as spring arrives. I have that clean out every closet, every corner, organize everything feeling. This year is no different. Everything that I see that is out of place I am putting it in place. Things that are in disarray, I am getting them in order. This holds true for my spirit as well. It is easy to get off track in this life that we lead. Often, we do so many things and get hooked up with people that we may begin to make poor choices, we start saying and doing things we just should not do and eventually, we find ourselves in a state of guilt and condemnation.

This week's encouragement is to help us get back on track and to leave that way of life for good. I have had countless people ask me, "Do you have to repent? You make mistakes too?" My answer is always the same, yes. I am not perfect. I just believe that God's Word is true, that if we ask Him to forgive us, He will. So, I repent and move on. The problem comes when we do not want to face the music.

I had a situation occur where I had made a major blunder. I mean a very stupid thing. That could have been easily dealt with from the onslaught of it. But, I chose to allow fear of the potential outcome to stop me from doing what "Jesus Would Do", so I suffered internally. I could not eat, I could not sleep well, I was afraid of what was going to happen next. Then, I heard the voice of God simply said to me,

"Sooner of later, you are going to have to grow up. You are going to have to become accountable to the decisions that you make. Whatever the consequences that come with those decisions, are what you will have to deal with. So, you better start listening to my word and doing what I say, because one of these times the consequences could be detrimental. It is children that do not want to take responsibility for their actions, but men and women of God do. It is a strong woman that says, no matter how much I don't like what may happen to me, I will take it since I created this mess."

What becomes very tough is when you do not want to deal with the truth, the fact that YOU created the mess that you are in. The hardcore truth of this matter is that I wanted to do things my way, and because I wanted it my way, I created a big mess. This has been an area of change that I have been dealing with over the past few months.

Many women deal with this same problem on a regular basis as they do not take direction well, we want to give direction, but we do not want to receive direction. Being married makes this a real tough issue with your spouse. If you find it difficult to do what your husband says, you have some work to do. You actually have a "PRIDE and SELFISHNESS" problem. Selfishness has to be put to death in your life; otherwise, you will only see things from your perspective and no one else's. Finally, my pride had to be broken. Pride prevents someone from being able to recognize that they are wrong about something. The Bible says that *"Pride always comes before a fall."* (Proverbs 29:23, Proverbs 16:18) Certainly, that is the truth. It is a long way down when you have built this tower of pride that you stand on.

The good news is that all of this can be rectified. Change is such a great thing if you receive the opportunity to change. The Bible tells us that we can *"cast our cares on Him, because He cares for us."* (1 Peter 5:7) The Bible also tells us that if we repent *"He is faithful and just to forgive us."* (1 John 1:9) Not only that, *"anything that we ask in the name of Jesus, God says He will do it for us."* (Matthew 21:22)

Action Steps for this Week:

1. Face the fact that you do not know everything and someone else knows more than you.
2. Write down the areas that you have been prideful and selfish. Burn or shred that sheet of paper as an act of never returning to pride and selfishness and ask God to forgive you.
3. Whatever the consequences are, know that you are strong enough to deal with them.

Week 23: Your Wealthy Place

Have you ever wondered when you will begin to live and be in your wealthy place? Many people are in search of this "wealthy place". Not just financial wealth, but health, peace, deliverance, and provision for every area of our lives. The big question is where is it and how do I get there?

Your wealthy place is where ever God tells you to go; it is the place that he has designated as the location where all of your provision will be for every area of your life. This place of provision cannot be a place that you select, but it is the place that God says is where you should be. Often times we want to choose our place of provision, somewhere familiar and comfortable. But our choice of a location is not going to get you to the wealthy place.

This happens with jobs, relationships, spouses, churches and many other choices that we have to make. We select something or someone based on things that are not spiritual but rather physical or emotional. So, instead of getting what God wants us to have we settle for less since we chose not to listen to the voice of God.

One great example of this is the prophet Elijah. God sent him to a "certain" brook. There, God said that all of his provision would be met. He would be sustained with water by the brook of Cherith and ravens would bring him flesh to eat. When that brook dried up, God sent Elijah to Zarephath, where a widow woman sustained him, not just any widow woman, but the one that God had already commanded to take care of him. (1 Kings 17:1-9) Just think if he had decided that he did not want to go to that specific brook or to that specific widow woman, but wanted to go to say the Red Sea or just any woman on the street, his provision would not have been there and he would have starved to death.

In order for us to get to a place of provision we have to make sure that we are open to listening and then being obedient to what God tells us to do. It is one thing to hear what God says, but it is a whole different thing to actually do what you heard.

Another great example is Abraham. God promised Abraham a son by his wife Sarah. It took 25 years to conceive and bear that son, but Isaac, was finally born. God told Abraham to take that same son and offer him as a sacrifice on the alter. So, Abraham being an obedient servant to God went to offer his son as a sacrifice. Just as he was about to slay him with a knife, God spoke through an angel and said, "Do not harm the boy, for now I know that you fear God, seeing that you did not withhold your only son from me. (Genesis 22:1-12)

Notice that Abraham was able to hear God and obey what he said. He did not argue with God and question him. If you continue reading into verses 13 and 14, you will find that God provided an animal for Abraham to sacrifice in place of his son. God never intended for Abraham to kill Isaac, but rather He wanted to test him to find out if he really trusted Him. The Bible says in verse 14 that Abraham called that place Jehovah Jireh or the Lord will provide. We have to make sure we are in the place where the Lord will provide, this is our wealthy place.

The question for us this week is: Am I in the place of provision, the designated place that God has set for me to have all that I need in this life? When you are in a place of provision, you lack no good thing.

Action Steps for this Week:

1. Ask yourself: Am I in God's designated place of provision for my life?
2. Seek God; ask Him what you need to do to be in your designated place of provision.
3. Finally, once God tells you what to do, do not question him, just DO IT.

Week 24: Relationships

Relationships – our friends, acquaintances, boyfriends, and spouses are each unique and rely on decisions that we make based on some type of measuring stick or value system. Some of us measure based on the Word of God while others measure based on television talk shows, family advice, co-worker experiences or even our own past experiences. But to truly have solid and divine, godly relationships, we have to depend on the Spirit of God and His Word only.

Many times we allow people into our lives by reason of obligation or poor judgment. The flip side of that is more times than not we do not allow people in our lives because they do not look like us, they do not do the things we like to do, or we simply cannot get past our own hang ups to surrender to God's leading of us into a relationship with someone. This week's encouragement is you will have the opportunity evaluate your current relationships as well as begin to follow God's lead on establishing new relationships.

The Bible says to know no man after the flesh (2 Corinthians 5:16) but we should know them by the Spirit. We are told to know a person by the spirit, their inner man, versus the flesh or the exterior things of a person. To know someone after the spirit means that you see their heart and how it is connected or disconnected to God. That is your first indicator of whether or not a person should even be considered to be in a relationship with you. If someone does not know God some conclusions can be drawn about this person: first, more than likely they do not live according to the Bible, they are pretty much living life as they please and whatever feels good is what they do. Second, what you may tell them about God and the Bible will not make much sense as they are in darkness and cannot understand the light of God. So, you have some choices that you need to make.

Where do you categorize people in your life? Does everyone that you have a relationship with get the same access to you and to your heart? A better question to ask yourself, do the people in my life even belong in a relationship with me?

Psalm 100:4 describes two levels of position as it relates to God and man. The scripture says; enter His gates with thanksgiving and into His courts with praise. The Old Testament describes a temple as having a gate, a court (often multiple courts) and the Holy of Holies. If we compare a temple our relationships with people we can use this same model.

In Bible days the Gate area is where the women, children and general public were allowed, it was a sort of what we would call a common area. The inner and outer court was the place where men and priests were allowed to come and pray, finally the holy of holies was the place that only the high priest was allowed only one time per year, where he would offer up the prayers of the people to God. This was a very sacred place.

When we establish relationships with people we should make sure that they fit into the place that God wants them in our lives. For example, our spouses should be in the holy of holies, they are the ones that should know our inner most heart issues. People that we work with perhaps will only be in the gate area as they are acquaintances and know basic things about us and our lives, the court area is in between the two, these people we spend time with, we may go on trips with them, they may be people we go to church with or even people we have know since high school. They are people that we take out time to get to know their heart and thus form a godly divine relationship. These people may (some of them) get into the holy of holies in our lives, but only if God says they should.

In the Holy of Holies of our heart are the secret things of God that he placed there. Our hearts are to be guarded at all cost (Proverbs 4:23) we are commanded to guard our hearts with all diligence. This same scripture goes on to say that out of the heart, flow the issues of life. Your heart holds your destiny; all the things that He wants you to accomplish are hidden in your heart. So, you should be cautious as to those you allow in that holy place, you have got to protect your destiny.

Action Steps for this Week:

1. Reevaluate your relationships. Look at each relationship and ask God, where does this person fit? Move them to the right position in your life. Know that God wants that person there for a reason.

2. Once you put people in their rightful places make sure that you cultivate your relationships, give them the appropriate time that they need. The Holy of Holies requires the majority of your time, while the people in the gate area require the least amount of time.

3. Married Ladies, many of you have people in the Holy of Holies that do not belong there. Your "best friend" and all your girls belong in the gate and court area; bring your husband back into His rightful place "the Holy of Holies", HE SHOULD BE ONE OF THE ONLY ONES THERE!

Week 25: Destined for Greatness

What is Life? Some say that it is the destiny that you are given and you cannot decide the outcome of it. Others say that life is the culmination of events that take place in one's time here on earth. Webster's Dictionary says life is the sequence of physical and mental experiences that make up the existence of an individual. I believe that life is a gift that God gives to each of us. What we make of it is all based on the choices that we make every day. This gift that we are given is to be used to create something so great that others can benefit from it.

Many of us view the life that we live as a day to day set of activities that may or may not have an impact on someone. God however views our lives as significant and important. The words that we say and the actions that we demonstrate should be reflections of the things that God has placed in our hearts. Every time we encounter someone, our heart desire should be to enrich the life of that person with words and actions. All too often we are in search of someone that can "give" us something. If we put our mindset in the place of giving to others, I believe that all of our needs will not go unmet, but God will make sure that we have more that enough!

As God's children we have a right to enjoy life. When God gave us the gift of life, He promised us goodness and long life, a life without destruction (Proverbs 3:2, Psalm 23:6, Psalm 91:16, Psalm 103:4). Moreover, He said that your own mouth is a well of life (Proverbs 10:11). Psalm 45:1 says that your tongue is the pen of a ready writer. We have been given the ability to create the life we want to have. So what, things have not gone the right way up until this point, but look at the bright side, you can change what happens tomorrow!

When you open your mouth and begin to say what you want to see in your life, you are creating your future. For example, let's say that the job you currently have is going no where really fast. You have reached an impasse. Promotion is not in your near future and you need a change. What do you do? Complain to your friends that your job sucks and you hate it, talk about your boss behind her back as if that will help, or do you start to make a positive declaration about what you see in your future. Perhaps something like this:

God I thank you that you have promised to bless me, and that you add no sorrow to my blessing. I thank you that you open doors for me concerning a new job. I thank you that my new job has opportunities for advancement, a great benefit package and a large salary. I thank you that you prepare me for my new job and when the door is opened I walk through into my wealthy place! Amen.

Action Steps for this Week:

Start saying what you WANT to see and stop saying what your eyes see and you will begin to create a life full of goodness and prosperity, not only for yourself, but for every person that you encounter each day.

Changing your words is difficult in the beginning, but as you get accustom to doing it, it becomes easier.

Week 26: Give up the Victim Mentality

Proverbs 17:22 says *a merry heart does good like a medicine: but a broken spirit dries the bones.*

Many believers walk around every day miserable wanting more for themselves, but not really knowing what to do to get a change in their situation. Our lives should be a culmination of experiences that leave us with a "merry" (happy) heart, sure you may have hit some bumps in the road and taken some left turns that sent you into a dead end, but ultimately, God has the ability to bring you back to the right path if you allow him. Sometimes people think they have gotten so far from the path that God has for them that there is no way to get back. So they continue life accepting whatever comes at them and not realizing that God is right there waiting on them to make the first move.

A broken spirit is a person whose heart has been damaged by life situations of death of a loved one, unforgiveness, loneliness, hate, injustice, broken relationships (perhaps divorce or a separation), financial struggles that you never recovered from, abandonment, or a child has left home or gotten married. Maybe things just are not working like you want them to at home. Because your heart did not have an opportunity to be healed from these things, you became broken on the inside. Each time something new happened to you that was not right, you internalized it and became more broken. The truth is each time a new hurt comes along, you become more and more broken and your insides are physically in a state of distress you may even be what doctors call depressed.

There is hope however. God's plan for you is so much greater than what you may be going through. The Bible teaches us that we have a great God. His greatness extends to us in which ever facet that we need. In this instance those with a broken spirit need Him to be a healer for them. Luke 4:18 says that Christ came to "heal the broken hearted." It is God's desire that you are healed from whatever is ailing you; no more do you have to be "broken".

Your healing can take place at any time. Once you decide that you are tired of living a life of brokenness you are ready for healing. The process is simple you ask God to heal you. Then, you allow Him to do it. You listen only to what His Word says about your life and your situation, you read and confess healing scriptures and you surround yourself with people that give life and the Word of God to you. Then, everyday thank God that you live a healed, happy and prosperous life.

If you are a person that suffers from brokenness or you know someone that does, I encourage you to help yourself and them make a change right now. Open your Bible and read Psalm 103:1-6 and meditate on it. I have included it here:

> *"Bless the Lord, O my soul: and all that is within me bless His holy name. Bless the Lord, O my soul and forget not all His benefits: Who forgives all thine iniquities; who heals all thy diseases; Who redeems thy life from destruction; who crowns thee with loving kindness and tender mercies; thy youth is renewed like the eagle's. The Lord executes righteousness and justice for all that are oppressed."*

Action Steps for this Week:

1. Bless the Lord (empower the Lord) with your words through worship, praise and adoration of Him.

2. Ask God to heal every area of your life. Even those areas that you have shut the door and intended to never reopen, let Him heal those too.

3. Allow God to do a work in you that only he can do by meditating and reading healing scriptures. Don't fight against the changes that he makes in your life.

4. Thank God that you are healed and whole in every area.

It is your right as a believer to be healed of any brokenness. Take back your wholeness today by allowing God to heal you from the inside out!

Week 27: The Best is Yet to Come

Have you accomplished anything this year? Have any of your prayers been answered? I want to take this opportunity to encourage you to stay strong in the Lord (Joshua 1:8, 9). The first half of this year may have been great for you, it may have been difficult, but one thing is for sure, we have more time this year to make it even better.

Hopefully, at the beginning of the year you wrote down goals in some specific areas: personal, family, job/career and church/ministry. Now that you have had some time to exercise your faith and work on these goals, it is the time to review them and see what progress has been made. Have you found yourself slack in working at any of these goals? There is no better time than now to get back on the wagon. Pull out that goal sheet you wrote back in January. Revisit what you wrote down. Determine in your heart to fulfill each goal and get moving.

If you have made some accomplishments I say wonderful and keep going. Once you establish a momentum, nothing will stop you from attaining all of your goals. Sometimes we need an accountability partner to help us stay focused, someone to push us when we get tired and someone to encourage us when we are discouraged by failures of the past.

Hab. 2:2, 3 says, "*Write the vision, and make it plain upon tables, that he may run that reads it. For the vision is yet for an appointed time, but at the end it shall speak, and not lie: though it tarry, wait for it; because it will surely come, it will not tarry.*" If you do not write down your goals, it is most certain that you will not accomplish them. Furthermore, you will forget what you want to accomplish.

One thing that has really been pressing upon me is education and self improvement. I know a large handful of ladies that have graduated from high school and are either doing nothing or working an $8 per hour job. It is time for you to reevaluate your 5 year plan for life. Unless you increase your knowledge, you will be stuck in your current situation. So, I encourage you to seek out a degree or certificate program. Check out some vocational schools, and talk with people who are in the field you are interested in and find out what you need to do. Do not be discouraged by finances or the lack thereof. Scholarships and financial aid are available and what you purpose in your heart to do God will provide the resources to make it happen. (Matthew 6:33)

Action Steps for This Week:

1. Review your goals from January, if you do not have any; write down goals for the following areas: personal, family, job/career and church/ministry.
2. Write down what you want to be doing 1 year from now, 5 years from now and 10 years from now.
3. Post your goals in a visible place in your home to remind yourself of your plans.

God is on your side and you cannot fail!

Week 28: Purge Yourself

Did you know that God wants you to live a wonderful and full life? God wants you to live a life of excitement and blessings everyday. In order to live this kind of life however, God has some requirements. One of those requirements is to live a sanctified life. Sanctified means separated or set aside. In order for us to be fully prepared for what God has in store for us, we have to make sure that we have separated ourselves from the things of this world.

To sanctify or separate yourself from the world means that there is a distinction between who you are and who the people of the world are. You serve God and the people of the world do not, therefore, there ought to be things about who you are and how you carry yourself that will allow someone to distinguish between you and those of the world.

Psalm 119:9 says that the way that you sanctify or cleanse yourself is to take heed of the Word of God. That means that God's Word replaces the things of the world that are on the inside of you. 2 Timothy 2:19-22 says that we must purge ourselves of all iniquity. Iniquity is that stuff that we do even though we know we should not do it, but we continue in it because our flesh likes it. Romans 12:1 and 2 also talks about renewing our minds. We are not to be like the world, but we are to be transformed by the renewing of our minds. We must put new information in and get rid of the old information that is not godly.

Once we have made a transformation in our lives and we begin to operate as pure and clean living vessels, we will have a greater opportunity to live out that "good life" that the Bible speaks about. Sure, we can continue to live mediocre and have short bursts of blessings, but why not live in an abundance of blessings every day of your life.

God desires 100% of you. If you allow Him to show you areas that you must purge, you will begin to see many more doors and windows open up for you. I encourage you to trust God in this area; He is ready, willing and waiting for you to take the first step so that He can bless you beyond measure.

Action Steps for this Week:

1. Make a list of areas in your life that you need to purge.

2. Ask God to help you purge yourself of those things.

3. Spend time meditating on the Word of God in the area of mind renewal and having the mind of Christ to replace that old information.

4. Look for God to open doors for you!!!!

Week 29: Encouragement is...

The word encouragement is a noun. It means support that inspires confidence and a will to continue. My prayer is that this encouragement does just that. It is my desire to inspire confidence in you and generate a will on the inside of you to press on forward in your life.

Sometimes the journey that you are on gets tough and cloudy, but that is no time to quit. That is the time to reevaluate where you are and make some adjustments. Perhaps you are at a point in your life where you are tired of being tired and now all you want is God and His Word. That is a wonderful place to be.

The Bible says in Matthew 5:6 "*that blessed are those that hunger and thirst after righteousness for they shall be filled.*" God's plan for each of our lives is so awesome and great that we cannot even comprehend the vastness of it. Your desire to get more of God puts you in a perfect position to receive more of the plan and desires that He has for you. The more of God that we desire the more He (God) is willing to give to us. God wants us to have everything that He has, but so many times we only take advantage of a fraction of Him. Jesus tells us in John 6:35 "*I am the bread of life: he that cometh to me shall never hunger; and he that believeth on me shall never thirst.*"

If you have come to the place that you really want your life to abound the way that God intended. I mean you really and truly have gotten tired of the way things are and want some real change; you have gotten to the point that you are hungry and thirsty for something that will fill you up. I encourage you to ask God for more of Him. He then will respond by saying, spend more time with me. How do I know this? Jesus told the woman of Samaria "*whosoever drinks of the water that I shall give Him (God's Word) shall never thirst; but the water that I shall give him shall be in him a well of water springing up into everlasting life.*"

Drinking God's water (the Word of God) will replenish us and revive us. Moreover, it will give us peace and power to go on. This water will be an endless supply of life that will flow from us to others. No more will we be tired and no more will we be ready to quit, but we will be invigorated and looking forward to another day to spend with our Lord and Savior! At the same time your life will be an example and a living testimony to others of what God can do!

Action Steps for this Week:

1. Set aside 30 minutes per day to read God's Word.
    a. Read a Proverb and a Psalm each day.
    b. Read a chapter from the Gospel of John each day.
    c. Read a story from the Bible that you may be familiar with but not real sure of all the facts of the story i.e. Daniel in the Lion's Den.

2. Make a journal entry each day about the time you spend with God.
    a. Write what you believe He is saying to you for your life.
    b. Write down what you want Him to do for you.
    c. Write down any thoughts or revelations you get from reading.
    d. Write down something you have learned from your daily reading.

3. If it seems strange at first that is okay. Keep going any way and watch God show you and give you all the desires of your heart.

Week 30: God Has Invested In You

God has made an investment in your life. The purpose for the investment is so that He can gather all of His children?

The word invest means to furnish with power or authority; to grant someone control; to endow with quality; to commit in order to gain a financial return; to make use of for future benefits or advantages; and to involve or engage emotionally.

When God placed destiny and purpose on the inside of you, He was making an investment into not only your future, but the future of the whole world. What you carry on the inside of you is meant to be something that would mark history forever. One of the definitions above is to make use of for future benefit or advantage. The gifts and talents that are in you were put there so that you could use them to be prosperous and be a light in this world. In the beginning of your walk with the Lord you had little knowledge of how to do certain things, but as you grew in the Lord and in stature, your knowledge base grew and now you know much more. You are now equipped to use your gifts and talents to benefit not only yourself, but those around you.

Look at another definition: to furnish with power and authority. When Jesus died on the cross and was resurrected, He told us that all power was in His hands. His sacrifice of death on the cross furnished us with power and authority. As a result of what He did we have been given the same Spirit and same power that Jesus had, therefore we are reaping the benefit of God's investment of Jesus.

God wants us to know that in each of us is power and ability. It is our job to take it, cultivate it and develop it. It was given as an investment; God's investment in us is for the purpose of redeeming this whole world. That means that what you have on the inside of you is important, valuable and precious!

Action Steps for this Week:

1. Read Matthew 25:14-30; parable of the talents. Read this parable and determine what type of servant you are for God.

2. Commit to using what is on the inside of you to benefit those around you.

Week 31: Passion on the Inside of You

Passion is enthusiasm, zeal, fervor, or intense emotion compelling action. What are you passionate about? What really drives you? What is it that you have on the inside of you that you could do without even thinking about it? That is your passion.

Women were created to do so many wonderful things. It is so important to understand that Satan would love for every woman to do NOTHING! When women gain momentum in their walk with Christ, Satan gets scared and sets traps and stumbling blocks in our pathway in order to stop us (John 10:10). We have to remain strong, rebuke Satan and keep moving (James 4:7).

The thing that you are passionate about is Satan's target. Whatever that thing is, that is what he is coming after. He will try every thing to get you to not do it, to stop you from thinking about it and more importantly, he wants to convince you that you cannot do it anyway. These are all lies! What God gave you a passion for is easy to do because God gave it to you; God ordained you to do it and God is with you every step, all the way to completion (Philippians 4:13). I pray that you do not give in to the pressures of the enemy but remain focused on the Lord.

I encourage you today to not stop pursuing the passion that burns on the inside of you. Even if it looks impossible, know that you are empowered to prosper. Jesus said in Matthew 19:26… with God all things are possible. That means that you can do anything. The only thing that can stop you from completing the assignment is YOU!

Action Steps for this Week:

1. Determine your passion.
2. Write out a plan to begin fulfilling your God given assignment
3. Keep moving toward completion and DO NOT QUIT! Quitter's never WIN the prize!

Week 32: Stay Strong in the Lord

Even in the midst of adversity you can stay strong in the Lord. No matter what happens do not let go of God's hand. When you are in darkness God can still see the path that you are on, but you must keep your hand in His hand.

These are some spiritual nuggets that I hold on to. Whenever I am faced with the unknown or situations that seem too hard for me to deal with on my own, I reflect back to the things that I know about God. I then begin to reassure myself that God will bring me through. Sometimes, I actually talk to myself out loud. I say things like: Lord, you will never leave me or forsake me (Hebrew 13:5); Lord, I thank you that my life is redeemed from destruction (Psalm 103:4); Lord, I thank you that you supply all of my needs (Philippians 4:19).

I keep a list of confessions near by so that at any given moment I can encourage myself in the Lord. Instead of an energy drink for a boost, I give myself a dose of the Word of God. I then feel refreshed and ready to continue my day.

The Bible tells us that David encouraged himself (1 Samuel 30:6). He did not wait for someone to come along and give him words of life to help change his mood or situation, but rather he took the time to remember what the Lord had done for him. David altered his mood and situation with the Word of God. You can do the same thing, you can encourage yourself when you are feeling low by speaking life giving words from the Bible.

Action Steps for this Week:

1. Write down five nuggets that you can post up at work and at home that you can use to encourage yourself.
2. When you start to feel low or distressed talk to yourself using your five nuggets.

Week 33: Overcome Fear and Failure

Fear and failure comes when you take your eyes off of your goals.

Have you ever established goals for yourself and set out to accomplish them only to get halted by a fear of failure? Did you say to yourself, "What if I mess up something or what if it doesn't work as I planned or what if no one thinks it is a good idea"? These are all phrases that a person says that has taken their eyes off of the final outcome.

I am reminded of Peter when he asked Jesus, "If it is you bid me to come and walk on the water." Jesus replied with "Come", Peter then walked on the water just as Jesus did. Then, when Peter saw the wind rise up he began to sink. His focus was taken off of Christ and placed on the circumstances around him (Matthew 14:28-32).

I encourage you this week to keep your total focus on God and the goals that you have set for your life. Do not make any situation or person your focus; these are obstacles that get in the way of your progress. Some of the people in your life often times do not see the vision that God has given you, so do not expect them to understand where you are going or what God has you doing. When your vision comes to pass it will speak for itself and all of the nay sayers will be silenced (Hab 2:3).

Action Steps for This Week:

1. Rid yourself of all fears. Ask God to help you stay grounded in faith.
2. Turn off your ears to those around you that say that what you are doing cannot be done. If God gave it to you, then you can do it!

Fear is the opposite of faith. God has not given you the spirit of fear, but Power, Love and a Sound Mind!

Week 34: Exercise Your Faith

Have you ever had one of those weeks where you felt like you woke up in a nightmare? When you went to sleep your world seemed fine, but when you woke up you just knew you had opened your eyes inside of a bad dream. The truth of the matter is that your bad dream is real and you are facing a real life situation that you cannot escape. Now is the time that you must exercise your faith, your belief in the Word of God. All the training and faith teaching you have stored up... it is now time to use it!

You keep asking yourself, what did I do to bring all of this upon me? You repent, you sing praises, you pray, everything you know how to do spiritually, you do it and still you do not have an answer as to why this is happening to you. The key to getting past this situation is looking past what you see and remembering what you know God has already said. You are a person that operates in faith not fear. Being a faith person means that you are *"pressed but not crushed, persecuted but not abandoned, and you are struck down but not destroyed"* (2 Corinthians 4:8, 9). Although you are dealing with some tough issues, you are more than capable of being able to handle the situation because you walk by faith and not by sight. Through all of this God will supply you strength and help you through this.

God's Word is able to handle any situation that we come up against but we must use it. It is not enough to know what the Word says, we have to be able to speak the Word of God over our problems and issues and then expect the Word of God to do what it was sent out to do (Isaiah 55:11)!

Action Steps for this Week:

1. Remember that God's Word is more powerful than the devil and more powerful than any problem that you may have.
2. Speak the Word of God over your problems and issues and expect to see positive changes.
3. When you are not sure what to do next... just stop and pray.

Week 35: Right Now Faith

Your level of faith will determine the outcome of every situation and circumstance that you find yourself in. Faith is whatever you believe put into action. There are things that we do day to day that require faith, but because we have become accustom to doing them, our level of faith in them is very high. For example, when you go to sit in your favorite chair, you do not question whether or not it will hold you or whether it will fall apart, because you have "faith" that it will do what it was designed to do, hold you. In the same way, we are to walk out our lives living by faith. When we drive in a car, ride in an airplane, speak in front of a crowd, deal with tragedy or triumph, all of it is to be by faith. Hebrews 11:1 says, *"Now faith is the substance of things hoped for and the evidence of things not seen."*

The main key to faith is that faith is ALWAYS right now. Not later, not when it gets here, faith is ONLY right now. So if you are not real sure about something being in faith, faith has not come yet, faith is on its way to you. But the moment that you begin to put your belief into action, faith has come.

Another example is an unsaved spouse, perhaps that person does not live by the Word of God, but you as the saved spouse put the Word of God into action. The book of Romans says that the wife can win the husband to the Lord by her demonstration of the Word, her example of Christ. So you speak life over your husband, you treat him with respect and you support him and you encourage him, more than that you do 1 Corinthians 13:4-8 you walk out love with him. Faith has come to you!

Faith comes by hearing and hearing comes only by the Word of God. Therefore, I encourage you to daily make sure that you are hearing the Word of God. Your faith will begin to grow and you will be able to see victory in your life. You will continue to move from one level of faith to the next. Each level of faith brings new trials, new situations and greater victories!

Action Steps for this Week:

1. Daily – listen, read or watch a Bible teaching, Word of God tape, video or the Bible.
2. Seek opportunities to walk in faith.
3. Be open to doing something you have never done before so that your faith can grow.

Week 36: Love

Have you heard people say that love is the most important thing that you can give someone? Love is important and is vital to all of our relationships. It is easy to love the people that we know well or those that we have irregular dealings with. But to love those that are "difficult" to love is another thing. As children many of us were taught to treat others as we would want to be treated. So, we strive to be nice, friendly, and cordial to people we come into contact with. How much easier would it be to operate in this principle if we understood love according to God?

1 Corinthians 13:4-8 (NIV) gives us a complete list of what it means to love:

"Love is patient, love is kind. It does not envy, it does not boast, it is not proud. It is not rude, it is not self-seeking, it is not easily angered, and it keeps no record of wrongs. Love does not delight in evil but rejoices with the truth. It always protects, always trusts, always hopes, and always perseveres. Love never fails."

We can clearly see that love is an action word. That means if we truly love someone we are "doing" something for them or to them. Loving people the way that God has outlined love, will guarantee us that our relationships will always be functional and beneficial to us. God's love gives us the power to have strong marriages and long lasting friendships. Only when we detour from God's love and substitute worldly forms of love do we have breakdowns in our love walk.

I encourage you to evaluate your love walk. Is it operating according to 1 Corinthians 13:4-8 or do you have some other form of love operating? Think about the people you interact with on a daily basis: coworkers, family members, church people, sales clerks, etc. how do you treat them? It is important to recognize that the principle of sowing and reaping is operating with love (Galatians 6:7). Whatever you put out will be returned to you. So, if you love little, you should expect to receive a little love back, but if you put out a lot of love, you should expect to get a lot of love back.

<u>Action Steps for this Week:</u>

1. Check out your love walk, are you demonstrating God's love to people?
2. Practice living in 1 Corinthians 13:4-8 with ALL people.
3. Expect to receive love from people every day as a result of you sowing love.

Remember that "*God is love*" (1 John 4:8) and He loves **<u>you</u>** more than anything!

Week 37: Money Isn't Everything

DOW, NASDAQ, $787 Billion Dollars…

That is the buzz, the economy, the stock market, banks without money, Wall Street falling apart, the USA as we know it is changing before our eyes. The media wants you to be worried and be fearful of what may happen to you and your money. Will you be able to take care of your family? What will happen to your job In light of this crisis? Will employers start firing people because they are loosing money? All these questions and more are being thrown at you everyday.

God on the other hand has a totally different perspective on the whole topic. He wants you to know that if you belong to Him, you will be able to endure the financial crisis. If you have put your trust in Him and you are operating in His system, you have no need of fear of what may happen (Matthew 6:33). You are protected and all of your needs will continue to be met (Philippians 4:19). What this means is that if you have crossed over into God's system of sowing and reaping, and you have been sowing seed into God's kingdom He is going to make sure that you reap even in times of financial crisis.

I want to encourage you to put all of your reliance on God. Put all of your trust, faith and dependence on Him, so that you do not have to worry about what is to come. As believers we should not have to worry about anything. We should recognize that even if the world around us falls apart, God will make sure that His people are taken care of and protected. I am reminded of Joseph in the Bible. He was sold by his brothers into slavery. He went from slave, prisoner, to second in command under Pharaoh. This did not happen just to make him a ruler, but God had a divine plan for his life. There was a famine in the land (a period of lack and insufficiency); Joseph was able to use his position to sustain his family, even though he had initially been sold into slavery.

God has things working right now in the spirit realm to make sure that all of your needs are taken care of. Even in this time of insufficiency in America; God can provide for us. The key is that we have to be found operating in His system. If we are not, then we should not expect to be sustained.

It is God's desire that you have a wellspring of abundance in your life, so much that those around you can benefit from your prosperity.

<u>Action Steps for This Week:</u>

1. Make sure that you are operating in God's system, which is seed time and harvest. Are you sowing seed (Tithes/Offering) to your local church? If not, make an adjustment and get into God's system, otherwise, there is no guarantee that you will benefit from God's goodness.

2. Read the whole story of Joseph including: his dream, being sold into slavery and becoming second in command under Pharaoh (Genesis chapters 37, 39-45).

3. Put your trust in God and allow Him to handle your financial situation.

Week 38: Comfort Zones

One of the best things about living in Minnesota are the wonderful weather changes. Last month we were basking in the warm sun and enjoying the beach and sand under our feet. Now with autumn in full force we can enjoy the leaves changing color and the beauty of fall. Before you know it we will be looking at the fluffy white stuff! Just when you have gotten comfortable with one season we walk into another.

Comfort is something that we all enjoy. It is our safe haven and a place that we are very knowledgeable. We know our limits and boundaries and what to expect. Have you ever asked yourself, why is our comfort zone the place that God wants to move us out of? Why can't God just allow us to be okay with living in our own comfortable little world where we call all the shots? We decide when and what we want to do and no one tells us "No"!

If we stay in our comfort zone we will miss the opportunity to increase and develop in life. Staying in your comfort zone causes your faith to stay stagnant and undeveloped. God pushes us out of our comfort zones by allowing us to face certain situations and circumstances of life. Remember the children of Israel. God used Moses to deliver them out of Egypt; God promised them a land flowing with milk and honey. When He freed them from Pharaoh they left Egypt with wealth and riches. They were on their way to new life. They found themselves in the desert, complaining every step of the way; this was truly a new place, one that was not known to them and not very "comfortable".

Although they were in bondage, they had become comfortable in Egypt. They knew when their meals were going to be served, when lights had to be out, where they would work each day and what they could do to be punished or rewarded. They were in total bondage, but they were very comfortable.

This is how it is in some of our lives. We have been in bondage to our jobs, working to pay the bills but not enjoying it. We have been in bondage to people; we care more about how they feel about us than how we feel about ourselves. We are in bondage to everything and we don't realize it because we are okay with it. Not until someone comes and tells us about what they see in our lives do we become aware of the bondage we are in.

I encourage you to open your eyes to your life and ask yourself, am I in bondage to anything? Have I become complacent in my day to day routine and have I put myself in a position to stop walking with God and growing in faith? Come out of bondage to people and things and enter into the freedom of God.

Action Steps for this Week:

1. Read Exodus 13:4-6; 19 and 20
2. Recognize areas in your life where you have become comfortable and complacent. Ask yourself; am I in bondage to anything?
3. Make a decision to be free in every area of your life and stay free!

Week 39: God is Faithful to You

When you think of the word faithful, what is the first thing that comes to mind? One popular answer is a relationship between a husband and a wife. Both expect one another to be true, authentic, reliable, close, and dependable, in other words faithful. The best answer to this question should be, God. God is the most faithful person we know.

Right now the world is in a sort of chaos. Many things are taking place it seems unreal, wars, stock market changes, housing market crash, job losses and much more. God however has promised us GOOD things. He has said in His Word that He would make sure that we are taken care of and that we should not worry about anything because He is faithful to His people (2 Thessalonians 3:3). This is good news! Knowing that God is faithful means that every promise in His Word will come to pass and all that we have to do is put our trust in Him.

My prayer for you this day is that you receive God's faithfulness in your life. He loves you and wants only the best for you. Even when you cannot see your way out of something and when you don't know what will happen next, just know that God is faithful and He will work it out!

Action Steps for this Week:

1. Read the following scriptures and make them your daily confession:
   Psalm 119:90
   Lamentations 3:22, 23
   Psalm 36:5
   Psalm 89:1
2. Look for God to demonstrate His faithfulness in your life.
3. Thank God for being faithful to you.

Week 40: Trust in the Lord

The year is not over. It is not too late to place a demand on the Word of God and put pressure on yourself to accomplish the things you set out to do this year. The Bible says that God is faithful. That means that what He says in His Word, He is reliable enough to do what He says. I made a list in January and I thank God that most of the things on my list are checked as completed and fulfilled. There are still a few things (big things) that are not done yet, but I am not giving up. I trust God and I believe His Word enough to know that He can fulfill each of them.

I encourage you to put all of your trust and faith in God. Trust Him with everything and surrender to the power of God over all the things you need to happen this year. Get rid of all doubt and simply yield to His Spirit at all times. He is able to do exceeding abundantly far above all you could ask or think (Ephesians 3:20). That means God will go over and beyond what you are asking Him to do, simply because He is God and He loves us!

Action Steps for this Week:

1. Find your list of goals/objectives for the year.
2. Daily put pressure on the Word of God – call forth with scripture everything that you are believing God for.
3. Do your part, whatever God tells you to do, DO IT!!!!

Stay strong; don't give up on God because He will NEVER give up on you.

Week 41: Your Relationship with God

What level of a relationship do you have with God? Is it shallow, the kind in which you only talk to Him when you need something? You find yourself in a bind and then you call on the name of Jesus. Is your relationship a fair weather kind, you talk to Him when things are going okay, but only when you have time, if it fits into your schedule; or do you have an intimate relationship with God, one that you talk to Him and He talks to you. You know His heart and He knows yours. You do not have to wonder if you are on God's mind, you know that you are.

Regardless of your relationship level, you should know that God has you on His mind all the time (Psalm 8:4). He is always looking for ways to bless you and increase your life (Psalm 115:12). Even right now God is making things happen in the spirit realm to make sure that you are empowered to prosper in every area of your life. There is a song called Friend of God by Israel and New Bread. The lyrics say:

Who am I that you are mindful of me?
That you hear me
When I call
Is it true you are thinking of me?
How you love me
It's amazing

Isn't it comforting to know that God has you on His mind and He is thinking of ways to bless you.

Action Steps for this Week:

1. Recognize what type of relationship you have with God.
2. If you find yourself with a shallow or fair weather relationship make some adjustments. Take out 15 minutes to talk with God and thank Him for everything.
3. Remember that God is always thinking about you and you are on His mind right now.

Week 42: The Needful Thing

What is the most important thing in your life? Is it your children? Is it your spouse? Is it your parents? Is it your job, or some other temporal thing? Did you know that if you have God and His Living Word you have everything that you need? By having God and His Word you can have security knowing that everything in your life will work out and you will have peace. Sure, there are some things that we must go through, but on the other side of the situation is victory if we give it all to God! I am reminded of Mary and Martha when Jesus had come with the disciples to their home. Martha was so discouraged and worked up that Mary was not helping her to serve, but rather sitting at the feet of Jesus. Jesus tells Martha that Mary has chosen the "needful" thing the good part. Getting God's Word is more important than anything else that we could put into our lives (Luke 10:38-42).

My encouragement for you this week is to put God in the center of your life and everything that you are going through. Forget about how **you** think you can handle situations, and allow God to deal with them all. Make a shift in your thinking... decide to respond like God. Give room to God to provide answers to all of your questions and accept the answers even if they are not the answers that you are looking for. In other words, be open to changes in your life and embrace them. God does know what you need and when you need it.

Action Steps for This Week:

1. Make the decision to put God first in trouble situations.
2. Open your mind to all that God has in store for you and make adjustments to your life.
3. Thank God that He is working in your life.

Week 43: Seek the Lord

Seeking the Lord is vital to the existence of everyone's life. To seek the Lord means to look for, to be in search of; or on the look out for. These definitions mean that we have to be actively looking, searching and on the look out for God. It will be impossible to get what God has for us if we do not on purpose seek him. Many times we face situations where God is the only one with the answer. We are looking high and low for the answers from people, television programs, newspapers or magazine articles instead of God. The Bible says in Matthew 6:33 that we are to seek first the Kingdom of God and His righteousness and all things shall be added unto us.

This is good news. Good in the sense that God is willing and able to give us all things if we simply seek Him first. We cannot be on the look out for money, the next big promotion, or even a spouse. Seeking these things are outside of God's order system. I encourage you everyday this week to seek God first. Ask Him what He would have you to do each morning. Then wait to hear His voice so that you can obey. Then, once you hear Him, obey immediately, because your life depends on it.

Action Steps for this Week:

1. Each morning ask God what you should do with your day.
2. Hear what God says and do it.
3. Expect God to add all things to you.

Week 44: What is Woman?

When I think of God's best work I think of the wonderful creation of woman. Unlike a man women possess distinct qualities and abilities that they did not get. What do I mean? We have the awesome ability to carry life, we can nourish and provide for our babies through the breast and we have the ability to adapt, complement and be suitable to our husbands (Genesis 2:18).

Today we have many messages being spoken about "the woman" and who she is and what her place is in society and the home. Many of these messages give a very skewed understanding of the true design and purpose of a woman and thus her situations do not get better, but rather worse because of this distortion.

God made us to be wonderful, powerful women of virtue and strength (Proverbs 31:10-31). Our design is so intricate that it is hard sometimes to figure us out, how we tick, and why we do certain things. Your complexity is what makes you so special and so unique. Inside of you are all the tools that you need to make your life great! Proverbs 31 is a scripture written by a mother of a young man. In this scripture the mother is talking to her son about what type of woman he should be looking for to be his "wife". She illustrates this woman of virtue by describing her strengths and abilities (or anointing). It is clear that the qualities that this woman has have been something that she worked on over a period of time. She was groomed and developed to be a woman of excellence.

Just like her, we have an opportunity before us to develop these same strengths and abilities in our own lives. It takes time to become a good business woman. Through some trials, some errors and failures you develop the skills you need to be successful. It takes time to become a "good mother", you may have to be mentored, read books and pray more often, but becoming a mother that is praised, takes development. In the same way it takes time to become a woman whose husband trusts her and is confident in her. Trust is earned and confidence is built; only time and wisdom can develop these qualities.

Action Steps for This Week:

As you read over Proverbs 31 this week, jot down the attributes that this woman of excellence possesses.

Ask yourself, "What makes her excellent?" As you write each thing down ask yourself how do I match up to her? Are you deficient in certain areas or have you mastered them? Have you become complacent in some areas? Being honest with yourself opens you up to allow God to help you make changes that will propel you into becoming a woman of virtue!

Week 45: Do Not Settle For Second Best

Compromise and settling for second best is not God's plan for us as believers. Have you heard people say that you should make compromises in life so that everyone benefits?

When you know that God has only the best for you compromise and concession are not options for you. When it comes to making decision and choices about things in life consider the ramifications of your decisions before you make them. Ask yourself, if I do this would God be pleased? Is my decision God's best for me or am I settling for second best? God's love for you is so great that He wants you to choose His best every time, even if it causes you to have to do something you have never done before or even if you have to go somewhere you have never been before.

I am reminded of what God said in the Old Testament. He says in Deuteronomy 30:19, *"I call heaven and earth to record this day against you, that I have set before you life and death, blessing and cursing: therefore choose life that both thou and thy seed may live."*

God's desire for us is to live a blessed and abundant life, He will not choose this for us, but He shows us clearly what we should choose, His best. Proverbs 10:22 tells us that the blessed life God has for us will not come with any burdens or misgivings but only empowerment.

Action Steps for this Week:
I encourage you to forget about compromise when it comes to life decisions. You are worth God's best and He saved you and has so much in store for you, more than you can imagine. Stick to what you know about God and His Word when you have to decide something. Then, once you have made your decision, stand firm and know that God is with you and will not leave you or forsake you!

Make life giving decisions this week. Weigh the pros and cons of situations with the Word of God and be confident with the choices that you make knowing they are based on God's Word.

Week 46: Set Boundaries

Do you sometimes feel as if you have lost time? Have you come to a point where you begin to recognize that you wasted lots of time and energy on things that were simply not important and you forsook the things that were important? When we chase after "things" we waste time. Time is one of our greatest assets, but it is also a limited resource that we must carefully use wisely.

Think of all the time wasted watching TV or talking about things that are simply useless to life. Wouldn't it be nice if we could rewind the clock and take that time back? That is not exactly possible to do. We sometimes allow people to use our time because we do not set boundaries. We operate from an unorganized and random lifestyle allowing anything at any time versus establishing a set time for specific activities that we must do and schedule time for things that we want to do.

What would your life be if you established a healthy set of boundaries for work, your friends, your family members and other activities? What about setting a time each night that you turn off your cell phone? What if you set a time to go to bed each night? Even turning off the TV one or two nights a week would help to set boundaries. These steps help to establish limits for your life and how you interact with other people. Making your time a priority demonstrates to other people that your time is valuable to you and you are not going to waste it.

Every moment of every day is precious. We have to see time as a valuable asset and something that cannot be wasted on trivial and petty situations or people. Look to each situation as an opportunity to find a solution versus perpetuate a problem. Remove yourself from situations that you cannot be a solution to; otherwise it will be a large time waster. Let go of difficult people as they will suck you dry of time.

Begin to see time on your side, watch windows of time open up in your life as a result of the boundaries that you have set for yourself and for other people to interact with you. Then, thank God that you have more time available to do the things that are in your heart to do!

Action Steps for This Week:

1. Evaluate how you spend your time. Are you watching lots of TV, going out with friends for hours on end? Do you sit around doing nothing and complaining? Take an inventory of what you do with the hours in your day.
2. Establish some new boundaries for your life: how much time will you dedicate to talking on the phone, text messaging, Facebook, and other communication tools; how much time will you dedicate to TV and radio; how much time will you spend reading/studying God's Word; how much time will you set aside for family activities?
3. Practice healthy boundaries by making some small changes first and then add larger ones as you become more comfortable with your new boundaries.

I pray that time is on your side and that all of the lost time in your life can be restored back to you (Joel 2:25).

Week 47: You are a New Creature

The Bible says in 2 Corinthians 5:17, *if any man be in Christ, he is a new creature: old things have passed away; behold all things are made new.* In order to be made new, a change had to take place. We had to come out of the world's way and come into Christ and His way, we had to move ourselves to "be" in Christ. Once we are in Him, the scripture says that old things have passed away and all things have been made new.

Now, do not look at your hands and feet to see if they look different, because this change is spiritual and not physical, therefore, you are not going to see any new physical changes, but on the inside of you, your spiritual man has been made new. Before meeting Christ you are like an attic filled with cob webs and old junk, but the moment you accept Christ as your personal Lord and Savior, you empty out that space. You send all the junk to the trash, you sweep out the cob webs and prepare that place for the new things that Christ has brought as a result of being "in Him".

True beauty is not what we wear, how we smell, the way our face appears or even the type of hairstyle we have. But true beauty is the image that one has when their life lines up with God and His Word. If we were to see true beauty, we would see Christ, we would see the characteristics of who God is iminating from the way that one carries themselves, by what they say and the actions that they make. We would quickly recognize this person, because they would be so different from the other people around them. In order to exude this beauty, change had to be made to this persons life.

Take a personal evaluation of yourself: First, have you accepted Jesus Christ as your personal Lord and savior? Are you in Christ and is Christ in you, not just by lip service, but does He dwell in you? Have you cleaned out that inner attic filled with the junk and the cob webs and allowed Christ to move in with all "His stuff"? If the answer is yes, praise God, you are well on your way to being transformed into that person of inner beauty that we recognize by seeing the character of

God in her life. If the answer is no, today is your day for change. Anyone can receive Christ, but they have to have a willing heart, a made up mind and believe that He is God.

Action Steps for This Week:

If you belive that today is your day for change, then say this prayer and receive Christ as Lord of you life.

Father, In the name of Jesus Christ, I ask you to forgive me of my sins. I believe that Jesus Christ died and was risen for me. I ask you to come into my heart and be my Lord and my Savior. I ask you to help me make the changes that I need to make to have a full life in you. I thank you for saving me now. Amen.

You are now well on your way to having an abundant life. Your next step is to begin attending a Bible believing, Word based church that can help you mature in faith and grow in the wisdom and knowledge of God so that your beauty can begin to come forth as a resulf of your new life in Him.

Week 48: You Do Not Have to Be Depressed

This week's encouragement is for those that have a sense of loneliness and depression especially during the holiday season. Perhaps it is not you, but you know someone that experiences depression and feelings of being alone. I encourage you to share this with them.

Newspaper headlines read, *"Depression High Due to the Holiday Season"*; as we draw closer to Christmas day, there are a large number of people that become severely depressed during this time. Where does it come from? Depression is a sign of an empty spirit, whether it has come due to the loss of a loved one, family problems, lack of finances or some other physical, social or mental strain, the empty spirit has to be filled by the Spirit of God. When your spirit is empty you will feel blue, you may attack people for no apparent reason with words or even actions, you feel lonely, you have no desire to do much of anything, and you throw pity parties on a regular basis and look for people to join you. The longer you remain depressed the worse it gets.

What can we do to get out of this state of depression? We have to be filled up by the Spirit of God; we need His Word to be active in us so that our spirits can be refilled. When Jesus was born the salvation of the whole world was in motion and the people of that time knew it. They knew that Jesus was born to save them. Well, just like He came for them, He is here for us right now. The best part about living right now is that we have the Holy Spirit which is God's Spirit with us at all times.

Matthew 1:18-25, is the portion of Jesus Birth where an angel appeared to both Mary and to Joseph at separate times and told them, Mary would have a son born of the Holy Spirit; you will name him Jesus (God Saves) (Emmanuel in Hebrew which means "God is with us"). Jesus knew He came to save the people of the world. In Luke 4:18, 19 He said, "*the Spirit of the Lord is upon me, because He [the Father] has anointed me to preach the gospel to the poor; He hath sent me to heal the brokenhearted, to preach deliverance to the captives, and recovering of sight to the blind, to set at liberty them that are bruised, To preach the acceptable year of the Lord."*

God has come to give you freedom from everything that wants to keep you in bondage including depression. He has power by the Word of God to free you from depression, and every ill of this world. You must simply ask Him to remove it from you!

If you have signs of depression I ask you to pray this prayer:

Lord, in the name of Jesus, I ask you to come into my life and deliver me from depression. I desire that my spirit be filled with your Word and your spirit and that I am free from the ills of this world. I accept you as Lord and savior of my life. Amen

Action Steps for this Week:

Every time feelings of depression rise up, begin to confess scriptures. These are your weapons against depression. Once your spirit is full of the Word of God, depression cannot come back in. You also must surround yourself with people that believe in the Word of God, people who can support you and continuously give you scriptures to keep you strong! God loves you so much; He wants only the best for you! This year instead of going into debt due to gifts, give the gift of Jesus to everyone!

Remember, Jesus is the ONLY reason for every season; it is only because of Him that we live, we move and have our being.

Week 49: Thank the Lord

Being thankful is a characteristic that is learned and developed. It is so easy to take for granted the simple things that we have been given.

Have you ever thought about the fact that without air you could not live? What about water, without it you would die of thirst; Did you realize that as you read this book there are those that cannot see it but have to have it read to them? The simple fact that you were able to wake up this morning and walk to your kitchen to make something to eat is a privilege that some people do not have.

Ephesians 5:20 says *to give thanks always for all things unto God and the Father in the name of our Lord Jesus Christ*; not just the "major" things, but ALL things. For the average person, we thank God when He gets us out of a bind, or when we have been asking Him for something that He "finally" gives us, a promotion or a healing. When was the last time you thanked God for being able to see the sun rise, for playing with your children, for being able to cook a meal for your family? Often we forget about the basic things that we have: our children, our spouse, our health and strength, our salvation, our home, having a sound mind and ability to love God. Daily, we should be thankful for everything that God has given us, the big things as well as the small things for all of them are important.

1 Thessalonians 5:18 says *"in every thing give thanks: for this is the will of God in Christ Jesus concerning you."* It is God's will for our lives to give thanks for everything, for it is God that gives us all these things (Matthew 6:33). We should make a concerted effort to set aside time daily to just thank God. Our thanking Him shows Him that we appreciate and love Him. Not only are we thanking Him for what He has done for us, but more importantly we are thanking Him for who He is in our lives, He is God! Being thankful is a characteristic that is learned. It is so easy to take for granted the simple things that we have.

Action Steps for This Week:

1. Set aside time to thank God each day.
2. Make a list of all of the things that you are thankful for.
3. After making your list thank God again for the great things He has done in your life!

Week 50: Time & Enemies

Have you ever considered how much energy is spent on hating people around us? For the majority of people there are at least two people that we just "don't like" for whatever reason. Perhaps they said something we did not like, they could have even stole something from us, maybe they left us for someone else, or they grew tired of us and decided I don't want to be in a relationship with you any more, or the most interesting one, they are just hard to love. Each of these reasons causes our bodies, minds and spirits to use energy that could be well spent on something else.

If we consider a day, there are 24 hours in it. Let's say that we spend 6 hours sleeping, which leaves 18 hours. We spend 8 hours working some form of job whether inside or outside of the home, that leaves 10 hours, we spend 2 hours preparing meals, eating and cleaning up, that leaves 8 hours left in the day. We spend at least 2 hours in a vehicle going from work, to school, to errands, to shopping, to entertainment and so on, that leaves 6 hours in the day. Next we spend at least 1 hour with God and 2 hours with the TV set, that leaves 3 hours left in the day, now if you have a family you give them 2 hours and if you care about yourself you spend 1 hour on you. My only question is where is the time available to hate someone? There is none!

A person we dislike or hate is considered an enemy. God has given us specific instructions on how to deal with enemies, and hating them is not the answer. God tells us that we should bless our enemies. Matthew 5:43 and 44 says: "*You have heard that it has been said; Thou shalt love thy neighbor, and hate thine enemy. But I say unto you, Love your enemies, bless them that curse you, do good to them that hate you, and pray for them which despitefully use you, and persecute you;*" God even continues in Psalm 110:1, "*The LORD said unto my Lord, Sit thou on my right hand, till I make thine enemies thy footstool?*" Now God is not saying that your enemies will be your footstool, but by praying for them, blessing them and doing good to them, you will reverse your anger, dislike and negative energy. That person will become a person of peace in your life due to your actions. No longer will they be a burden to you, but you will see that God can turn that relationship around.

One very familiar scripture says thou prepare a table before me in the presence of mine enemies: thou anoint my head with oil; my cup runs over (Psalm 23:5). This scripture says that God will prosper you and increase you in the presence of your enemies. He is not going to wait until every one likes you, but right in the midst of the uncomfortable place of blessing, and praying for those enemies, God is going to bless you!

You can spend so much time and effort doing things to yourself and to other people that your health becomes affected. You start getting headaches, your blood pressure rises and your heart starts to act funny. But why allow your health to fade? God has purposed for you to do great things and if you are not around, someone else will have to get your assignment!

Having right relationships with people is one very important way to establish the character of God in your life, loving your enemies is what God would want you to do.

Action Steps for This Week:

1. Check your relationships, who do you "hate" or dislike?
2. Ask God to forgive you.
3. Go to that person or those people and reconcile with them.
4. Pray for those that are on your "hard to love" list and watch God perform a miracle in your relationships!

Week 51: Accomplishments

I am excited about all of the accomplishments that were made this year. I know that this was a difficult year for some at the same time, but right now is the start of something brand new. We have a new year right around the corner and we can make it exactly what we want it to be. How do we do this? We have to decide what we want and go after it.

I encourage you to look over your life and think about what you want. Do you want to change the way you look? Do you want to change the job or career that you have? Would you like a larger or simply a different home? Do you want to get married and start a family? Do you want to make some changes with the family that you have? Whatever it is you have the power to make the changes with the words that you speak. Decide right now to take control of your situations by speaking what you want to see rather than what you currently see. Use the power of your tongue to create the life that God wants you to have (Proverbs 18:21).

Once you have spoken it do not change your words or your thoughts. Know in your mind and in your heart that you have what you have said (1 John 5:13-15). Then, expect God to do whatever necessary to manifest His goodness in your life! Remember that what you invest is what you will be able to withdraw. What that means is whatever you put into this exercise is what you should expect to get out of it. If you put little effort into it you will only get a little, if anything, out of it. But if you put much effort into this exercise, you should expect to get a whole lot. As a matter of fact, expect God to perform miracles in your life this year.

Action Steps for this Week:

1. Use your mouth as a tool for life deposits by speaking positive words over yourself.
2. Challenge yourself to only say what God says about you. Remember that you are making an investment in your life.

Week 52: Set Goals and Achieve Them

Let us thank God for this year. Thank Him for the good things, the not so good and the things in between, we thank Him for every victory and every trial. Why, because with each situation that we encountered, we grew in faith. We now know more than we knew last year. We are stronger, wiser and most of all we are closer to God.

As we go into the New Year I challenge you to write an Action Plan. In order for a specific thing to be understood and put into motion, you must write it down. Statistics show that those that write down their goals and objectives are much more likely to see them come to pass than those that do not. Hab. 2:2, 3 says, *"Write the vision, and make it plain upon tables, that he may run that reads it. For the vision is yet for an appointed time, but at the end it shall speak, and not lie: though it tarry, wait for it; because it will surely come, it will not tarry."*

Action Steps for this Week:
Write down an Action Plan for the following areas:

1. Your personal life: Do you want more for next year?
2. Your family: What do you want for your family this year? Do you want to be closer & spend more time together?
3. Your service/ministry at church: How about this year you fit everything around God and His desires for you at your church.
4. Your job: Perhaps a promotion, change in careers or back to school!!!!

You have made it through another year and God is ready to carry you through the next, His Word says *"Be still and know that I am God"* (Psalm 46:10). God already has everything figured out, if you just stand still and let God be God. Proverbs 3:5 says, *"Trust in the Lord with all your heart."* Let him fight all your battles, and WIN them for you.

Acknowledgements

I thank God for giving me His awesome power and ability. It is only through and by Him that this book was written. I thank Him for using me to create this work that can benefit women all over the world to transform their lives.

I thank my closest friend, my life companion, my husband Connell for his encouragement and support, you truly do complete me! I thank my children, Daniel, Joshua, Naomi, Ashley, CJ and Cierra, for their creative ideas, honesty and patience; you are all a blessing from the Lord.

I thank my parents for giving me life and a strong foundation. I appreciate you and love you more than you will ever know. I acknowledge my wonderful mom, I encourage you to always remember that God is on your side; you are an example of a woman of excellence, strength and virtue.

I thank every woman that I have ever come into contact with. It is through our interactions, casual conversations, challenges, triumphs and fellowship that my life has been enriched and empowered, each of you have blessed my life and made this book a reality. My prayer is that through this book you will be strengthened, encouraged and empowered to do EVERYTHING that God puts in your heart!

I thank every woman that encourages another woman as a result of this book. It is only through the development of our own personal strength and faith that we can encourage and empower others. I hope that the words within this book have made such an impression on you that you want to share it with every woman in your personal network.

Again, thank you all, be strong, keep your faith and be encouraged!

About the Author

Cerise D. Lewis is a wife, mother, chemical engineer, business woman, teacher, mentor, tutor and friend.

She has been given the awesome calling to minister to the needs of women. She is fulfilling this calling at the Church of Minneapolis, through her work in the women's ministry. Monthly, she teaches and encourages women through the Women's Day Program and empowerment classes. In addition, she is the president and founder of the Pink Purse Project, a non profit organization that provides encouragement to women through the gift of a purse and encouragement seminars. The organization assists women in developing confidence, self worth and personal growth.

Cerise Lewis lives in Minnesota with her husband Connell F. Lewis, Sr. they have six children: Daniel, Joshua, Naomi, Ashley, CJ and Cierra.

I hold my time on Long Lake like an amulet. It is a charm washed with the amethyst of an autumn sunset on calm water and softly fogged by the opalescence of cedar smoke rising through still night air. In distress, it quiets me until my life is the silence of owl's flight.... It resonates with the heartbeat of a bear .... And always it takes the shape of a waxing gibbous moon, and glows with bits of light captured from that moon which hung above my camp, reflecting the better half of fullness.

from "Confluence" by Kate Boyes, Winner in the Prose Division

❖ ❖ ❖

At night I release all the fish
from my hair. Shore-leaved from me,
they grow big as zeppelins,
swim down the airwaves
of a dozen all-night oldies stations,
head out over the city
leaving trails of smoke and pearls.

from "Fish Story" by Pamela Miller, Poetry Winner

Other Books by Whitney Scott

Freedom's Just Another Word
Alternatives – Roads Less Travelled
Prairie Hearts
Words Against the Shifting Seasons
Listen to the Moon
Dancing to the End of the Shining Bar